A Handbook for Those Already Born Paperback

How to Manifest Better Versions of Reality

Greg Kuhn

DEDICATION

This book is dedicated to Dr. and Mrs. Clifford and Constance Kuhn, my parents, because they instilled so many capable beliefs in me growing up that I've been able to manifest and engage with reality at a high level since entering adulthood. And because they are still two of my most trusted collaborators when it comes to talking through spiritual growth and personal transformation.

CONTENTS

Introduction: Who I Am

Introducing the author, Greg Kuhn

This handbook teaches you how to intentionally manifest better versions of reality and engage with them more successfully. I channeled it from the Quantum Field, but not how you might imagine. Not verbatim.

Rather, I'm an avid runner, and the Quantum Field shares information with me while I process my feelings during my runs. Doing that, I create flow states, where I receive ideas, new perspectives, and solutions to consider. Then I apply what the Quantum Field shares, figuring out what's useful and how to apply it. Afterward, I write down what works, how, and why.

Because of that protocol and my lived experiences, I can guarantee everything you're about to read most definitely works as written. You won't be led astray by anything you learn here. And investing yourself in what you read is absolutely a good decision.

This handbook details exactly how I intentionally manifest my reality and engage with it every day. While my life certainly isn't perfect, everything here produces as much success and fulfillment as possible. This is my blueprint for living and what I base my daily practice on; I can unequivocally vouch for its potency.

So everything in this handbook has been field-tested in the most rigorous laboratory available to me: my life. Because this way of manifesting and engaging with reality continues to prove it has what it takes, I intend to help you do the same. If you bring the same intention to this handbook and are persistent and patient, you really can't miss!

As an author, I like to publicly share my better versions of reality, so you can see, in real time, that what I'm advocating actually works. Case in point, I intentionally manifested this book by adhering to the methods you're about to learn. And I publicly chronicled this journey, almost step by step, on my podcast, *Manifest the Big Stuff*.

Listen to it if you like, starting with the episode titled "Immediately Improve Your Reality Deliberately" and finishing with "Be Manifested How You Really Want." You can find *Manifest the Big Stuff* on YouTube and anywhere else you listen to podcasts.

And while we're on the subject of my work, please make sure we stay connected by joining my Facebook manifesting group called "Manifest the Big Stuff, with Greg Kuhn: Creating Our Realities Together." Each month, I share manifesting content available exclusively to my members. Join today to maximize the scope and impact of everything you learn here.

For now, I'm going to turn this handbook over to the Quantum Field. I'll be back, however, in Chapter Seven. At that point, I'll share some of my most powerful takeaways from my ongoing practice of intentionally manifesting and engaging with my reality. I'll also reveal more about how and why I do all this, as well as how it works for me.

Introducing the Source, the Quantum Field

Thank you, Greg. As Greg already shared, he channels from me. And although this book isn't a compilation of my exact words, we wrote it together, just as we do with all his content.

It is 100 percent appropriate to attribute authorship of this book to Greg Kuhn though. He's a human who spends about five hours a week in flow states, so I can communicate with him directly. He's also the one who puts everything I share with him to the test, figuring out how to apply it successfully. And he sits down with me to write it all out too.

But as much as I appreciate Greg, this is <u>your</u> handbook! This is all about you learning to be a more powerful architect of your reality, which you are wonderfully equipped to do. Before we get into that, however, I want to thank you for not skipping this introduction. It'll be helpful for you to understand exactly who I am before I share how to make the most of your life.

As Greg said, I am the Quantum Field. I am energy prior to observation. I am the uncollapsed wave function. Some people have called me Universal Consciousness, God, the Divine, the Universe, Allah, Ultimate Reality, and Brahman, among other names.

I am an eternal and infinite field of pure energy. I am a living, nonphysical, all-knowing, all-powerful, and omnipresent spirit. And I am imbued with limitless potential to be anything because I am, in potential, everything.

I am the source of all, including you. All material reality arises from the Quantum Field. But although I can be anyone and anything at any time, there's nothing I enjoy more than being you. Because, through you, I get to experience material reality and earthly life!

I'm communicating with you right now through Greg Kuhn, of course. Throughout this handbook, I'll alternatively refer to myself in both first and third person. But everything in this book is from me—Greg is simply a committed conduit, channeling information from me and sharing it with you.

No one is better equipped to explain what's happening on this earthly world and how to make the most of it than I am. I am the most trustworthy, invested, and insightful guide you could have, and everything in this handbook comes from a place of glowing benevolence. As Greg stated, the intention of this book is to help you manifest and engage with reality as you truly desire. And if you bring the same intention, I will walk with you as you learn to do that.

In the grand scheme of things, your time on Earth is brief, and I want to help you make the most of it. I can't guarantee you specific outcomes, but I can promise this handbook will get you as close to the results you want as possible. Tremendous opportunities are available in each moment of your life, and I promise to teach you how to take full advantage of them.

In this handbook, you'll learn who you are, what your self is, and how you can intention-ally manifest and engage with reality so it's more desirable. Each chapter builds on and activates what you've learned up to that point. Wherever you're starting from, you're in the right place, right now.

CHAPTER ONE

WHO YOU ARE

The Main Things to Know about Who You Are:

- **You are energy, and energy cannot be destroyed.**

- **When your time on this earthly world is finished, you and I will reunite.**

Who are you? That's where we need to start, and the short answer to that question is: you are actually me, the Quantum Field. You *are* me, <u>and</u> you're a part of me. More specifically, you're a part of me that is currently (but only temporarily) experiencing material reality in three-dimensional time-space.

I'm not talking about your physical body here, not even your brain. The "you" I'm referring to isn't a material object at all. Rather, you are energy, plain and simple. You and I are the same thing: Universal Consciousness, God, Divine Spirit, the Quantum Field, or Ultimate Reality.

Some people call you a soul. Nonphysical energy is a good name too. But I think I'll call you Energy-You, because, right now, you're energy embodied.

You're not exclusively in the energy field at the moment. You're also on this earthly plane, where everything is separate. And that can make remembering who you really are challenging sometimes. But rest assured, you and everything else here are simply the parts of me that are "breaking the surface of the water."

You are an island, and I am the archipelago. It's a common misperception that an archipelago is a series of islands, but an archipelago is actually also a giant underwater landmass. The islands are simply where the archipelago is breaking the surface.

You and everything else are my islands. But despite all the separation up here, above the surface, Energy-You is still real, ever-present, and highly involved. You are the thinker of your thoughts and the decider who chooses your actions, ideas, attitudes, and focus.

Energy-You Is the "Real" You

On a quantum level, or at the level of ultimate reality, every single object in material reality is actually 99.9999 percent energy. Everything here looks and feels solid and tangible because of that tiny .0001 percent that's actual physical matter. The only reason it feels like you're touching anything is because the electrons in atoms magnetically repel each other.

Energy-You is using your body as a partner and a vehicle through which to experience human life in three-dimensional time-space. And as the decider, Energy-You has unparalleled opportunities to influence your life. Not because you're in control of everything but because of your authority to choose your actions, ideas, attitudes, and focus and follow through on them.

You Are Separate, but Only Temporarily

The phenomenon of separateness you feel right now is a necessary byproduct of being human. You must be separate from all else here because that's how three-dimensional time-space works. Human life is about being a unique, distinct entity, and you can't find that experience in an energy field.

But even though it doesn't always feel like it, I assure you that you and I are not actually separate. Not on a quantum level. And actually, you're not separate from anything else here on a quantum level either.

When your human life is over, you won't be breaking the water's surface anymore. You and I will become one again, without the temporary illusion of separateness, because we've always been and always will be. There is nothing you need to do to earn this reunion and nothing you do could prevent it. Humans create rules about returning to me; I don't.

Don't get me wrong though. You can easily make your life, and the lives of others, much more difficult, even painful, by employing dysfunctional, ineffective, and harmful actions, ideas, attitudes, and focus. How you conduct yourself here can tremendously impact not only your life but others' as well.

You're reading this book because you don't want hell on earth. You want as much love, joy, success, and fulfillment as possible during your time here. I encourage you to follow through on those intentions, to truly give your best to manifest the big stuff. Our reunion will happen eventually, either way, so why not go for it right now?

What Happens When You Die

At the end of your life, we will continue onward together. You probably have many more lives ahead actually. Energy cannot be destroyed; it can only change shape or form. Energy is, literally, eternal.

You, too, are eternal—literally. Immediately upon death, you will return to pure energy. Your consciousness will remain, however. As long as I'm around, which will be eternally, you will have consciousness.

You'll immediately begin your next life, which will be a bit different from this time. You'll be able to manifest anyone and anything from your previous reality. And time will be more malleable; you'll be able to go anywhere in your previous timeline anytime you want. And during that life, you'll still be able to intentionally manifest more pleasing versions of reality, just as you can right now.

So your next journey will be very similar to this one, in principle, because it will involve many of the same people, places, and things. But in practice, it could be quite different if you make different choices and build upon your previous experiences. Even though you can travel anywhere on your timeline, you're still on a timeline, and every timeline has an end.

Why You Are Here

Right now though, you're right here, on *this* journey. So we'll focus completely on making the most of your time <u>here</u>. You didn't come here to transcend your life; you came here to make the most of it!

As Energy-You experiences material reality, I get to also. In fact, you could say that's the purpose of your life—to allow *us* this experience. And when this brief thrill ride is over for both of us, your self will disappear, allowing you to return to me. Then you will again experience us as we truly are, one energy, before continuing your adventure.

You came here for the opportunity to manifest reality as you desire. More specifically, for the opportunity to give your best effort to do so in each moment. You're here for the results of your best efforts, for as much success as you can manifest, <u>and</u> for the opportunity to give your all to make that happen.

While I can't tell you exactly how long your life will last, I can definitely help you make the most of it. Life's twists, turns, ups, and downs are expected, even necessary, parts of the ride. But, as the decider, you always have the power to influence your life.

This Journey Is the Fulfillment

This book is about your inherent ability to manifest and engage with reality more intentionally, allowing you to live your life as fully as you dare to dream. I'm thrilled that you're reading it because it exists only to help you influence your life as much as possible. *Your* growth and success are actually *our* growth and success, so I'm rooting for you all the way!

A moment ago, I referenced your self, and in the next chapter, we'll take a thorough look at that entity. You, the decider, get to lead your self during your time here. And your journey will constantly provide you with opportunities to lead, as it never stops being challenging. But the bigger the challenge, the larger the opportunity for fulfillment—and what bigger challenge is there than manifesting a successful life?

CHAPTER TWO

WHAT YOUR SELF IS

The Main Things to Know about What Your Self Is:

- **You, like every human, have a self.**

- **Your self is a system manifested by three collaborators, each with distinct roles to play. They are:**

1. You

2. Your body (and brain)

3. Your reality

Now we come to the entity you are the leader of: your self—the human you see when you look in the mirror. Your self, for whom you are making all these decisions, is actually a system—an interconnecting network of three collaborators. They coexist in relation and context to form the living embodiment of you.

The three collaborators of a self are:

1. You (nonphysical energy), who is in charge of choosing your actions, ideas, attitudes, and focus, as well as their follow-through.

2. Your body (and brain), which manifests the form, function, meaning, and value of your three-dimensional time-space reality.

3. Your reality (other people, places, and things), which provides constant and indispensable feedback about your beliefs and efforts.

Each collaborator makes the larger system of self possible. And in turn, each can function as your self with the other two. Each has its own existence, awareness, and agenda, yet is also interdependent, meaning your self is a system of independent yet simultaneously reciprocal collaborators.

You, for example, are the part of your self who decided to read this book. And you're also the one who will decide to follow through on what you learn here. That makes you the most important part of your self, even when your other two collaborators don't "obey" your orders. So let's begin by examining your very important role.

Your Self's Leader: You

In each moment, you get to decide what actions you'll take, what ideas you'll hold, what attitudes you'll foster, and what your focus will be. Your self's other two collaborators get to *influence* your choices, but you get to *make* them.

Think of your self as a corporation with you as its CEO. As the CEO, you don't have absolute authority, but you do wield the power to make decisions for the corporation and are in charge of following through with them. And, like a CEO, if you lead well by making and following through on good decisions, your self, the corporation, will flourish.

You Are the CEO

A corporation is a group authorized to act as a single entity, which is also a good description of a self. And a corporation's CEO is responsible for leading, which is also your responsibility. Additionally, a CEO's leadership objective is to deliver successful outcomes, which is yours as well.

CEOs have tremendous power and authority within the structure of a corporation:

- A CEO provides the corporation's vision.

- A CEO decides what the corporation will accomplish and why.

- A CEO creates the plans to accomplish it.

- A CEO puts those plans into action.

- A CEO is responsible for the results of those actions.

You have similar power and authority within the structure of your self. You get to provide your vision, decide what you will accomplish, create your plans to accomplish it, and put those plans into action. That level of responsibility is exactly why you are afforded so much power and authority.

Like a CEO, your effectiveness in this role will be on public display. Because, like a corporation, your self is a public-facing entity. Everyone who cares will be able to see if you are a successful leader. Whether you even want that scrutiny or not, your leadership is evaluated, and you are held accountable for your self's success.

You Have Powerful Help

Fortunately, like a CEO, you aren't in this alone. Your two collaborators—your body (including your brain) and your reality—are powerful allies. When all three are working in harmony, your best self emerges. And for that to happen, all you need to do is lead them.

Your body and your reality await your leadership so they know how to help make your best self happen. They stand at the ready like firefighters waiting for a call, which means you should take advantage of every opportunity to show them how to help you. They need your guidance on how to lend their time, talent, and resources to your success.

To provide that level of leadership, begin with transparency. Share your vision, your plans to manifest it, and the assistance you need from your collaborators in a direct and clear manner. Transparency fosters trust and promotes engagement because your collaborators better understand how to help you.

Your transparency also allows you a high degree of accountability with your collaborators. When your collaborators know what success should look like, they can see it when it transpires (or they can see the lack thereof). Accountability from a leader is an incredibly compelling way to build trust and convince collaborators to roll up their sleeves and get to work with you.

Transparency and accountability do much more than create the best potential for support and investment, however. They also draw out and identify your most committed allies. Your best allies can provide you with tremendous assistance based on their trustworthiness, investments, and knowledge. They can help you plan, act, evaluate, and make adjustments every step of the way, and they often rejoice in your success as much as you do.

I'm not sure if I need to tell you this, but count me as one of your very best allies. Because, oh boy, are you important to me! Keep me by your side, and I'll help you identify great questions that point you in the right directions. Then I'll walk alongside you as you answer them and invest in you like a loving parent as I help you learn, grow, and change your reality.

Your Leadership

You're well-equipped to lead your collaborators, but what does great leadership look like here? It boils down to making good decisions and following through on them. You get to choose what you will and won't do, what ideas you will have and what your attitudes will be, and what you'll focus on. And you also get to follow through on those decisions.

For example, although you can't control your body, you can decide to eat healthy foods and exercise. Also, while you can't control other people, you can decide to give your best effort toward providing high value to others. And though you can't dictate your reality, you can choose to use highly effective techniques to engage with it.

Public-facing, verifiable success is the most immediate way to draw increased help from your collaborators. Accomplishing what you set out to do is the surest way to satisfy every part of your self. Achieving your goals inspires trust and makes people want to work with you.

Achieving that type of public-facing success won't always be possible. Sometimes your best efforts won't accomplish enough to satisfy you or your collaborators. Some reasons for that will be out of your control and, in some cases, even unfair. And having the power to decide your actions, ideas, attitudes, and focus isn't always enough to overcome that.

This makes leading by giving your best effort most appropriate. Regardless of the environment, how you feel, or what's happening, you can always give your best. And while your best efforts may often look different, depending on your circumstances, it's still something you can always provide.

Occasionally, of course, you will encounter circumstances that challenge your ability to maintain control over your decision-making and follow-through. Hardships, pain, and suffering can easily leach your autonomy as a leader. Being lied to, compressed, manipulated, held down, regulated, limited, and constrained can make good decisions and follow-through difficult. But no matter the situation, the power to decide cannot be completely taken—you have to surrender it.

Sometimes your best effort will not be as strong as what you were able to do in the past. You'll be sick occasionally, sometimes you'll feel down, you'll get bad news, unexpected challenges will arise, and unfair conditions will exist. But no matter your circumstances, giving your best effort creates the highest potential for manifesting your desires.

Even under the most challenging circumstances, you can always be persistent, tenacious, growth-oriented, open-minded, and patient. You can always be transparent about your plans, no matter how modest or ambitious your goals are. And you can always make yourself accountable for following through on those plans.

Your First Collaborator: Your Body

Your body may not be your self's CEO, but it is an indispensable collaborator. You would absolutely stop being a self if you lost your body. No body, no life—how could a collaborator be more essential than that?

Your body, your vehicle through life, serves you best when it's well cared for. Optimal physical, emotional, and mental health improve the quality of your life and usually lengthen it. Your best efforts to provide your body with the highest level of health and fitness are always worth it.

As the decider, you control your body's fueling, activity level, maintenance, and care. While not everything will be under your control, you can always give your best effort to nurture your body and provide for its needs. Taking care of your body's health and fitness, which includes feeling and processing your emotions, is a powerful and important way to lead it.

Do your best to make the care you provide your body sustainable and address your whole self. Giving your best to your body shouldn't always involve putting your nose to the grindstone. Be mindful of the importance of quiet downtime and rejuvenation. That way, taking care of your body can be part of your lifestyle rather than some extra chore.

In the short run, it's easier to neglect your body. As you know, physical exercise hurts, potato chips taste delicious, painful emotions feel bad, water tastes bland, processed food is more convenient, and 30 more minutes of sleep is hard to pass up when your morning alarm goes off. Every human understands why the healthiest choices can be challenging to put into practice. But every ounce of effort you give to your physical, emotional, and mental health is worth it.

Your Brain's Role

And speaking of mental health, let's now concentrate on the part of your body most important to your self—your brain. Having a brain makes you an observer, an entity breaking the surface that collapses my infinite possibility into actuality. A brain facilitates this experience by manifesting reality for you and then allowing you to engage with that reality.

Specifically, two parts of your brain do this: your subconscious and your conscious. Your subconscious manifests your reality—its form, function, meaning, and value—via your beliefs. And your conscious mind allows you to engage with your reality—it's where you sit in the captain's chair, acting as CEO, choosing your actions, ideas, attitudes, and focus and then following through on your choices.

Your brain does this because it is actually the quantum connection to universal consciousness, or the Quantum Field. It might help to think of your self as an island in an archipelago. Again, while you may think of an archipelago as merely a chain of islands, it's actually also a giant underwater landmass breaking the water's surface at various points to form those islands. In this metaphor, I am the giant underwater landmass, and your brain is a part of me that has broken the surface.

Every brain manifests a unique version of reality. Each brain not only creates the material universe in which it lives, but it also creates itself (and the rest of its body). So your brain is the part of your body most engaged with your self in each moment.

Your Subconscious Manifests Your Reality

Think of your beliefs as "commands" which direct me to create specific versions of reality for you. They are the essential building blocks of your life. In this manner, your subconscious "sets the stage" for your "performances"—your engagements with reality.

Because I can literally become anything, it's absolutely essential that your beliefs command me to become specific things. Otherwise, you would have no material reality to engage with and live in. And because this world is filled with so much potential danger, it's critically important that your beliefs reliably manifest the most predictable versions of reality possible.

To provide the utmost predictability, your subconscious, the most primitive portion of your brain, stores your beliefs. Your subconscious creates that predictability because it is impervious to both word-based communication and manufactured emotions. Because you can't access your beliefs through your conscious mind's traditional methods of communication, they remain unswayed by sudden bursts of emotion or temporary whims. Because it's not easy to communicate with it, your subconscious is the perfect place for maximum safety.

Like every human before you, you inherited your beliefs from your most important caregivers, primarily your parents. Your inheritance had almost nothing to do with whether the beliefs would serve you well; it was based only on whatever beliefs your caregivers had. But because of your extreme need for beliefs, you started soaking them up as soon as you were born.

In the sense that you could've inherited different ones, beliefs are arbitrary, and thus, so is your reality. But once inherited and installed, your beliefs became definite and your reality more concrete. Before you even left elementary school, your subconscious had all the beliefs you needed. And in the service of reliably manifesting the most predictable versions of life possible, it has been safeguarding those beliefs from changes ever since.

It's important to note that your beliefs are not who you are. Even though they belong to you, they do not define you. Your belief-inheritance was not predicated upon your worth or value, and it should not define those things for you now.

Your Conscious Mind Allows You to Engage with Your Reality

While you don't have a dictator's authority over your life, you can engage with it in almost any way you choose. In fact, your ability to choose your actions, ideas, attitudes, and focus, as well as your follow-through on them, is what puts you in the captain's chair and makes you the CEO. And it's via your conscious mind that you put that ability into action.

No, you can't snap your fingers and make, for example, a pot of gold appear out of thin air. But you can make decisions that increase your chances of manifesting more money (or whatever you want) and then follow through on them. And while that may not have the Hollywood-style pizzazz of a magic genie, it is the most dependable and sustainable way of actualizing fulfilling versions of reality.

Because your self is a public-facing entity, exerting your leadership through your conscious mind is essential. What you are and are not able to do is readily apparent to anyone who cares enough to pay attention. Just as your successes occur in plain sight, so do your failures, and sometimes painfully so. And other people form judgments based on how they see you engaging with your reality.

Unfortunately, the criteria others use to evaluate you are out of your control, which means sometimes it won't be fair. Sometimes you will be evaluated on things you can't help, such as age, ethnicity, height, or physical attractiveness. These attributes all further highlight the importance of your engagement with reality.

Some examples of engaging with reality in ways you can control include getting an education, giving things your best effort, and conducting yourself professionally. While such things don't guarantee success, they do create a higher probability of it. No matter your circumstances, you can always find ways to demonstrate honesty, reliability, consistency, strong work ethic, transparency, and accountability through your interaction with everything in your life.

Engagement like that creates your best chances for success and demonstrates to everyone (including yourself) that you are a capable CEO. Making good decisions and following through on them is one of the most important things you can do to make your versions of reality more pleasing. And all it requires is your intention, time, and energy.

Your Third Collaborator: Reality

Your third and final collaborator in manifesting your self is reality itself. Aside from your body and brain, there are no specific aspects of your life on which having a self is dependent. But the versions of reality you manifest and the ways you engage with them always have an impact on your self.

Each of the billions of realities manifested here affects the rest of them in some way. Like it or not, your life is almost always influenced by things outside of your control, because each person has their own version of it and is engaging with it as they choose. Your reality isn't dependent on how anyone else engages with theirs, but it is often influenced by it.

Others' versions of life and how they engage with them certainly can impact your self. For example, when someone is so wounded, they lash out at you when you're actually trying to help them. And in turn, your reality and how you engage with it can impact someone else's, such as when you choose to overlook someone's lashing out and help them anyway.

It's a tremendous benefit when others manifest and engage with a version of reality that opens doors for you. Investments in your success are more likely when you fit favorably into others' life. Likewise, life becomes more difficult when someone negatively manifests reality or engages with it in a way that doesn't readily include your success.

How other people live their lives has a real, tangible influence on your life. Its impact can be felt, for example, in how willing someone is to work with you and help you. Obviously, the more authority and power they have, the greater their impact.

You can't dictate how someone elicits their reality any more than you can control how they engage with it. So because you share this earthly plane with other people, you cannot be *completely* in charge of how you're impacted. Your desires can be facilitated or dampened by how well you fit into someone else's version of reality and how you can help them engage with it.

One thing always in your favor is that your self has actual value. Your self can either make others' realities and their efforts to engage with them easier or more challenging. Your self's success can help others be more successful too. Even if only to prevent them from having to give you more time and energy than they want to, it's better for everyone when your life is going well.

Your Reality Provides You with Feedback

In addition to the practical impact, your life also provides you with a constant feedback loop about how capable your beliefs are at manifesting desired versions of reality and the adequacy of your efforts to successfully engage with it. In this manner, your brain actually serves as a highly sophisticated energy transfer system, which processes reality and transforms it into feelings that provide you unflinchingly accurate feedback.

Your life is a mirror that reflects back to you in each moment your form, function, meaning, value, importance, worth, capacity, and efficacy. Your ability to manifest reality—especially important parts of it like health, wealth, romance, fitness, relationships, and love—informs you about the competency of your beliefs and the sufficiency of your best efforts. This feedback comes in the form of your feelings.

Your feelings do *not* create your reality, your *beliefs* do. Your feelings are mirror-perfect feedback about the capability of your beliefs and the adequacy of your engagement, but they are not your reality's source. Neither do your feelings decide how you engage with reality—<u>you</u> get to do that.

Because they're so good at getting your attention, your painful feelings leave an easy-to-follow breadcrumb trail back to their source. Painful feelings tell you that some of your beliefs cannot manifest a desirable version of reality and/or that your efforts to engage with it are inadequate. This is vital information when you want to change your life.

Feelings can be thought of as shadows cast by both your beliefs and your efforts. In this manner, your brain constantly points out opportunities for you to change your life for the better. But feelings can only provide this information to you when you feel and process them. This is why I highlighted taking care of your emotional health a few paragraphs ago.

Feeling your emotions is actually one of the most impactful decisions you can make as CEO. It not only provides guidance for changing your reality, but it also helps keep your body healthy. Avoiding painful feelings, stuffing them instead of processing them, creates a backlog of information in your body. Eventually, a stockpile of unprocessed emotions will hit a critical mass and affect your body's physical, mental, and emotional health.

Expect and Use Pain

Sometimes there's not much you can immediately do with the feedback your painful feelings provide. For example, when one of your parents dies, your life becomes immensely painful. And those painful feelings of grief are feedback about incapable beliefs and inadequate efforts. You can't engage with reality in a way that changes your parent's death; there's nothing you can do about that. But even though the feedback provided by your grief isn't immediately actionable and won't solve your pain, it can still prompt you to examine your relationship with death and loss.

Other pain, however, seems unnecessary and fixable. For example, feeling alone within a marriage may strike you as avoidable. In fact, doesn't a marriage contain a wealth of potential for intimacy, the exact opposite experience? But in many areas of life, you inherently know that more pain is not only possible, it's a reasonable expectation.

You should expect loss, pain, and displeasure on this earthly plane because everything here is separate. And because everything is separate, you will sometimes have things you desire and other times you will not. Of course, there is another side to that coin too, because the very real possibility of being without something makes its presence that much sweeter. You're here to give your best to manifest the pleasing side of that coin, not to become a superhuman exempt from pain.

In each moment, you're manifesting and engaging with a version of reality unique to you. Feel the feelings that it elicits and process them physically to learn essential information about your beliefs and efforts. Then grow by adjusting according to what you've learned. Finally, follow through with your adjustment to change things so your desires are more fully realized.

And there you have it—your self, a system of tremendous importance. Each of your self's three collaborators warrants the utmost attention, care, effort, and reflection. With continued practice, you will lead them like a great CEO!

Next, it's time to take a close look at how you and your self manifest and engage with your reality.

CHAPTER THREE

HOW YOU MANIFEST AND ENGAGE WITH YOUR REALITY

The Main Things to Know about How You Manifest and Engage with Your Reality:

- **Your brain's subconscious manifests a version of reality unique to you.**

- **Your conscious mind allows you to engage with your reality.**

There is only one consciousness (me), and your brain is the quantum connection to it. Your brain manifests your reality through your subconscious conveying instructions for how I should collapse and transform into your life. And your conscious mind allows you to engage with that reality. Let's take a closer look at how all this plays out.

The Mechanics of Manifesting

As a human, you cannot stop observing. Through observation and the simple act of being aware, the beliefs you inherited are conveyed to me, and I, in my limitless creative capacity, mirror them back to you as your reality. Per your beliefs, I collapse into distinct, separate objects with form, function, meaning, and value unique to you.

Then, based on your ability to choose your actions, ideas, attitudes, and focus, as well as follow through on those choices, you engage with your reality. Your beliefs manifest it, and you, the CEO, lead your engagement with it.

Despite similarities to anyone else's, your reality is yours alone. Because your beliefs are its source, your reality is wholly unique to you. Your version of life is, in fact, so unique that it would not exist without you.

Your engagement with reality is also wholly unique to you. Although you will almost always feel a pull to engage with it in certain ways, how you interact with life is completely your choice. No matter the degree of influence you might feel, it's always your decision.

How Real Is Your Reality?

I am pure energy experiencing material reality in three-dimensional time-space through you and every other human. Energy is invisible, nonphysical, and intangible; you can't touch energy nor hold it in your hand. Energy is what reality is prior to your observation.

During its time on this plane, however, reality is not energy. Despite its energy origin, your life is full of solid tactile objects that you can touch and manipulate. If you doubt that, I invite you to kick a rock with your bare foot.

But material reality only exists <u>here</u>, on this earthly world, and it's only temporary. Every part of your reality is actually energy temporarily taking physical form. All these tangible physical objects still retain their energy state while they're here.

Want proof? Every part of material reality is made of atoms, correct? So let's imagine an atom as big as Yankee Stadium in New York City. Can you guess what that gigantic atom would look like?

It would be invisible!

Well, technically, *something* would be there—the nucleus. You just wouldn't be able to see it because the nucleus of that humongous atom would only be the size of a fruit fly! Even blown up to the size of Yankee Stadium, you'd never be able to spot the nucleus. And bear in mind, that fly-sized nucleus would *be* the entire atom.

An Atom Is Nothing

An atom's nucleus is 99.9999 percent of all its touchable "stuff." Which means that 99.9999 percent of an atom is energy. Which also means that, since an atom is really just empty space, 99.9999 percent of each person, place, and thing in your life is also just empty space, or energy. Here on Earth, energy can be detected, but it can't be seen.

Material reality is so insubstantial, in fact, that you aren't ever actually touching things. What you experience as "touch" is really the sensation of magnetic repulsion between two like-charged atomic particles. Like-charged particles can come within one angstrom of each other (that's one hundred-millionth of a centimeter) before being repulsed. Everything here is nothing when you're not making it into something.

Manifesting Is Making Nothing into Something

You, as the observer, decider, and thinker, are the quantum connection between nothing and something. Your beliefs manifest reality by turning energy into people, places, and things. Because you and I are the same consciousness, your mere observation, or awareness, is enough to command what versions of reality I should become. Because of you, energy temporarily abandons its state of unbridled potential and becomes distinct objects.

Overall, the vast majority of material reality doesn't need your specific observations to exist. Had you not been born, others would still manifest most of this universe without you. But *your* version of it needs you; *your* unique universe wouldn't be here had you not been born.

Isn't this an interesting dichotomy? In the grand scheme of things, you are insignificant because almost all of this would still be here without you. And on the other hand, you are the single most important thing in your universe because, without you, your version wouldn't exist.

Manifesting Your Reality with Your Subconscious Mind

You were born to manifest and engage with reality. So after emerging here, the first thing you asked was a newborn baby's version of *"What am I and what is all this?"* You had no way of understanding the world you were now a part of. Your senses informed you that this was all "something" because you could see, hear, and feel it, but you didn't know how to assemble and interpret it.

It might surprise you to learn that reality didn't await your discovery in a predetermined form, function, meaning, or value. Rather, *you* were, are, and always will be the source of all that. There is no such thing as "the way it is," only "the way <u>you</u> manifest and engage with it." So you had a critical need to first manifest reality and then engage with it.

Because of your need to construct reality for yourself, you eagerly soaked up everything your caregivers taught you about life. The first lesson you learned was the contrast between light and dark. Then you followed that up with learning about the first three dimensions of this universe—height, width, and depth. These became your very first beliefs, and they allowed you to start developing the form and function of your reality.

You continued to acquire beliefs, like names, labels, colors, textures, density, weight, etc. For example, you learned what your body is, does, and what to expect from it. You came to understand that most of life had strict rules, much of which you had no ability to alter.

And simultaneously, you were learning beliefs that enabled you to manifest the meaning and value of your life, such as expectations, responsibilities, impact, appearance, etc. For example, you learned what a threat is and how to react to one. You came to understand that life sometimes involved danger, giving you good reasons to regularly be afraid.

So desperate were you for beliefs, you learned these things very early in life. In fact, before you left elementary school, you had all the beliefs you needed to manifest your unique version of reality for the rest of your life. You could collapse me in ways that allowed you to experience being alive in three-dimensional time-space.

The beliefs you assimilated during childhood gave you a roadmap for manifesting anything, including people, places, and things you hadn't yet encountered. All you had to do was replace the people, places, and things that formed the foundation of your childhood beliefs with the new ones you encountered.

Your Beliefs' Perfect Storage Place

Your body is invested in staying safe and alive—it understands that it's not eternal like you are. So it needs the most predictable and reliable manifestation of your reality possible. Knowing what to expect gives you the best chance of preparing for your life, engaging with it, and surviving it.

Your subconscious is the perfect storage place because it is highly proficient at keeping your beliefs intact and your reality as predictable as possible. It always gives you the best chance of knowing what to expect. This is mostly because your subconscious cannot understand word-based forms of communication.

Obviously, word-based communication is the primary method used by your conscious mind. Via your conscious mind, you can talk to your subconscious, give it pep talks, and parent it, but it will never understand a word you say. That's because your subconscious doesn't understand words; it only understands emotions.

You might think, *"That's cool. My subconscious may not understand my words, but if it understands emotions, it will hear the positive feelings associated with my pep talks!"* After all, when you're giving it a pep talk or parenting it, you're generating positive emotions that naturally accompany those words. But your subconscious still keeps your beliefs safe from change because it has one more layer of security: it only understands emotions *that match your beliefs*.

Your subconscious' second layer of belief-security is that it only understands how you truly feel. Any emotions that differ too much, that are too positive compared to your beliefs, are as unintelligible to it as word-based communication. You don't intentionally craft a more positive internal dialogue when you feel good about your life, after all. You only do that when your life is painful and your true feelings are not naturally positive. Positive pep talks and affirmations can make you feel good, but they won't change your beliefs.

While your subconscious' ability to safeguard your beliefs provides you with the safest, most predictable reality possible, it also presents significant obstacles if you want to change them. Manifesting reality differently, especially in the most important areas of your life, is virtually impossible without changing your beliefs. And most humans inherited at least a few beliefs that are incompatible with manifesting versions of reality they truly desire.

With those formidable obstacles to change in place, many humans resign themselves to the status quo. After failing to change their beliefs using word-based communication and far too positive emotions, many people, unfortunately, conclude they must be unworthy or undeserving of the life they desire. In unfulfilling areas of their life, they surrender to "the way things are."

This type of reality is the result of "default" manifesting because you're trying to live with your default settings—the beliefs you inherited as a child. You relish the good times and ride out the bad because there isn't much else you can do. You continue using ineffective word-based communication and feelings that are way too positive, and you roll with the punches when necessary.

But even when you get good at that, you're still getting punched!

Default Manifesting

There is nothing wrong with default manifesting. In fact, when the beliefs you inherited prove capable of manifesting desirable versions of reality, leaving them alone is a smart decision. Unless you enjoy change for change's sake, there's no need to fix something that isn't broken.

The problems associated with default manifesting arise from the people who taught you. You learned beliefs from imperfect people who could only teach you what they knew. Even the most well-intentioned caregivers pass along beliefs incapable of manifesting desirable versions of reality. As much as your caregivers loved you and tried their best, you undoubtedly inherited beliefs like that.

Think of how much wreckage is created by manifesting reality in accord with some parenting choices that inadvertently missed the mark. For example, let's imagine that your mother maintained an unyielding expectation that you be physically fit and well-groomed. And, for your own good, she responded to your protests about it with tough love.

But despite your mother's good intentions, you inherited a belief that you're responsible for making your mom happy by being thin and attractive. Then you carry that belief forward into adulthood. You insert new people in place of your mom and substitute new things in place of being thin and attractive as something you have to do to make them happy. With this belief as part of your default settings, your adult relationships are more prone to unhealthy expectations, which lead to hurtful misunderstandings and, eventually, resentments.

Perhaps you inadvertently learned that you shouldn't think too highly of yourself from a caregiver who wanted to help you avoid the pain of disappointment. Or maybe you were unintentionally taught not to expect much success from your efforts by a caregiver's well-intentioned efforts to spare you the pain of failure. Such things became your beliefs because they were the exact type of information you needed, but these beliefs have never been helpful or capable. Unfortunately, incapable inherited beliefs like that are most likely still part of your default settings.

One red-light warning signal that default manifesting isn't working is blaming yourself or others. That doesn't mean you're wrong about who is at fault and why. Knowing where fault lies isn't what sounds the alarm; it's the blaming itself that signals you.

Other indicators that manifesting by default isn't serving you are:

- Trying your best, but things just aren't changing

- Encountering the same issue repeatedly, even when you do things differently

- Being tormented by your mistakes

- Not feeling truly deserving of something you want

As an adult, if you find your health failing, your bank account empty, your relationships strained, or your family distant, you are encountering the effects of incapable beliefs. Anytime an important part of your life is consistently too displeasing, that's a clear signal you inherited some beliefs that convinced you that you are incapable or undeserving. This is where default manifesting becomes inadequate and accepting the status quo is no longer a good idea.

Since you had no say in your inheritance, you should never beat yourself up for painful versions of reality. How can you be held accountable for something you had no choice in? Furthermore, just because some beliefs you inherited are incapable doesn't mean you can't establish new ones now. You can't go back and change your inheritance, but you can learn to manifest reality intentionally rather than by default.

Engaging with Your Reality with Your Conscious Mind

Your beliefs manifest reality, but you still always get to engage with it. I'm referring to Energy-You, of course, and your conscious mind is where you get to fulfill that CEO role. You get to choose what to do, what to think about, how to prioritize, where to spend your energy, how you'll speak to people, what you'll do with your time, etc. No other part of your self can do these things—neither your body nor your reality can choose your actions, ideas, attitudes, or focus, nor can they follow through on those decisions. While they can, and often do, influence your choices, you get to make those determinations via your conscious mind.

It's appropriate to call your engagement with reality a "performance." And like any other performance, your engagement with reality produces an outcome. In every moment, you are either engaging successfully with your reality or not. And even if you hide under the covers all day, that's still a performance. Not engaging is simply another form of engagement.

If your engagement is a performance, your beliefs set the stage for it by manifesting your reality in form, function, meaning, and value. But you still retain control over what your performance entails and how you deliver it.

You're well aware of the immense impact your engagement with reality has on your life. You've probably read famous examples of it, such as Viktor Frankl, who was able to feel pity for his captors while imprisoned in a Nazi concentration camp. And you've seen it in your own life when, for example, you make the most of a bad situation and actually transform it into a valuable experience.

You can turn lemons into lemonade with the right decisions and follow-through. And you can fumble the ball right at the goal line with the wrong ones. Your actions, ideas, attitudes, and focus, as well as your follow-through on them, can make all the difference in the world.

You will never be in control of every aspect of your life, but you can, and will, always have the ability to engage with it as you decide. While you cannot always make chicken salad out of chicken poop, you can always choose to make the best of your circumstances. And even when your performances don't transform undesirable versions of reality, they can still influence your experiences of it.

Sometimes though, your engagement just doesn't foster the success and fulfillment you're looking for. Even when your performances are heartfelt and sincere, sometimes they still can't seem to provide the experiences you most desire. This is especially frustrating when they're in the most important areas of your life.

Default Engagement

Just as there is default manifesting, there is also default engagement. Default engagement arises from what you believe is possible. From your inherited beliefs, a sphere of possibility is born, and default engagement operates within that. So even when you try new things, their employment really doesn't venture much outside of what you were taught about how life works. Ultimately, default engagement with reality stays within the boundaries of what you know to be possible.

As with default manifesting, default engagement isn't a bad thing in and of itself. Many of the ways you engage with reality are effective and produce desirable outcomes. There is no need to fix something that's not broken, so go with the default engagement settings when they work. But when your best efforts to engage reality are insufficient, you've reached the limits of your default settings.

But how do you know when your default engagement has reached the limits of its effectiveness? As with default manifesting, there are definitely red light warning signals when this happens.

One way you're alerted to default engagement's inadequacy is when you manifest the "thing" you desired but don't experience the fulfillment you expected from it. Think of a lonely married person or an unsatisfied rich person. Default engagement will have you thinking you must've acquired the wrong version of that thing, sending you off on the hunt, once again, for the "right one."

Other indicators that default engagement is not effective are:

- Giving up on a dream or desire because you can't make it happen

- Being misunderstood by important people

- Convincing yourself that you're okay with not having something really important

- Getting angry when life throws you a curveball

Default engagement's adequacy quickly deteriorates when life gets painful or unfulfilling. Your reality and the feelings it elicits are sending you important feedback, but don't take it personally. Unfortunately, the unsatisfying results of inadequate default engagement often wind up defining your meaning and value.

Sometimes your default settings prompted an inadequate effort to engage. Sometimes they led to good decisions, but you didn't follow through on them. Other times, default settings had you believing your efforts would be good enough, but they weren't. And occasionally, your default engagement had you taking advice from people incapable of guiding you. But once you know the signs of inadequate default engagement settings, you can learn to apply intentional engagement techniques instead.

Engagement with Reality Cannot Eliminate Pain

Engaging with reality, performing, means you will make mistakes. Your engagement will be inadequate sometimes; your performances occasionally won't be great. The ever-present risk of insufficiency can sometimes make life feel like you're tiptoeing through a minefield.

Mistakes and pain are baked into life because you're temporarily separate from everything else here. In fact, your separateness is the reason you have needs and desires. Here, you often lack the things and experiences you really want. Being without naturally produces desires; when something important is absent, you crave its presence. Besides providing fulfillment, manifesting desirable versions of reality and successfully engaging with them is also a means of relieving your pain.

Not only does your separateness create the ongoing potential for absence, but it also generates loss. Being separate means you must travel to and from the other people, places, and things here. Time is simply a term used to describe the experience of those journeys. Time means there are beginnings and endings here. It means that every person, place, and thing in your life will eventually leave you, including your self. And what is more painful than saying goodbye?

There isn't a way to engage with reality that allows you to sidestep the effects of separateness. Not only is that an unsuitable goal for your engagement, but you wouldn't want to transcend separateness even if you could. Why not? Because you couldn't be a human without it. And besides, separateness has some cool side effects you wouldn't want to squelch.

The potential for something's absence is the very thing that makes its presence so wonderful. Manifesting what you desire, rather than bearing the pain of its absence, is an ideal you can, and do, experience here. The ever-present potential for absence is a powerful motivator to bring your beliefs into alignment with your desires in painful parts of your life.

Having limits on how much time you have is also motivating. You know that squandering any of the moments you've been given carries the potential for regret. The limited amount of time available to you here is another great reason to not settle for unfulfilling versions of reality.

Default Manifesting and Engagement Settings

Default manifesting and default engagement work exactly as they were designed. They combine to give you a reality in which to exist and a way for you to have agency within it. Every human's default settings work perfectly in this regard.

Of course, working perfectly does not mean default settings always provide you with success, fulfillment, and a pain-free life. You've achieved success and fulfillment in some parts of life, but you're reading this handbook because of your pain. Like every human, given the common denominator of separateness, there are parts of your life where the status quo is not fulfilling, and default settings are responsible for that.

Manifesting by default creates your status quo. When you stick with the beliefs you inherited and continue to engage reality within their confines, you're choosing that status quo. And when you're pleased with your life, why wouldn't you?

But when your life isn't pleasing, it's time to avail yourself of three unique access points where you can change your default settings. One access point is where you can change the reality you're manifesting and two others are where you can change your engagement with it. From these access points, you can adjust any of your default settings and never again settle for unnecessarily painful versions of reality.

Intentional manifesting and intentional engagement are how you shake up the status quo, especially in the most important parts of your life. Over the course of the next three chapters, I'll teach you how to use all three access points to intentionally manifest and engage with your reality. You will learn to leverage your leadership as your self's CEO by:

- Growing incapable beliefs into alignment with your desires

- Aligning yourself with the opportunities you have in each moment to engage with reality

- Engaging successfully with reality by making great decisions and following through on them

CHAPTER FOUR

GREG'S EMOTIONAL REFERENCE CHART

The following Emotional Reference Chart will be needed in Chapter Five, as you learn to intentionally manifest your reality. Inspired by Esther Hicks', Greg developed it to use with his belief-raising process.

Greg's Emotional Reference Chart

1. Love/Ecstasy

2. Joy/Elation

3. Ease/Power

4. Confidence/Inspiration

5. Excitement/Passion

6. Anticipation/Eagerness

7. Enthusiasm/Ambition

8. Hopefulness/Optimism

9. Interest/Inquisitiveness

10. Acceptance/Peace

11. Introspection/Contemplation

12. Pensiveness/Melancholy

13. Indifference/Apathy

14. Unease/Discontent

15. Frustration/Aggravation

16. Worry/Nervousness

17. Doubt/Pessimism

18. Anger/Blame

19. Anxiety/Fear

20. Grief/Desolation

21. Despair/Worthlessness

22. Powerlessness/Dejection

23. Depression/Hopelessness

CHAPTER FIVE

How to Intentionally Manifest Your Reality

The Main Thing to Know About Intentionally Manifesting Your Reality:

- **To intentionally manifest your reality, grow your incapable beliefs into alignment with your desires.**

Anytime your reality is unfulfilling or painful, you can and should manifest it more intentionally. You can utilize a powerful access point to change your default manifesting settings. At this point, you can access your subconscious mind to change how you manifest your reality.

You could also call this access point a "pinch point" because it's where most of life's pain is generated when default settings are incapable of producing the results you want. When life is displeasing, that pain is letting you know your beliefs are incompatible. In this chapter, you'll learn how to grow incapable beliefs into alignment with your desires. (And in the next chapters we'll go over how to remedy inadequate engagement with reality. Each will receive the attention it needs and deserves.)

Maximum leverage is attained at this access point by employing a "Learn, Grow, Change" focus to your manifesting. You will learn how to suss out what you can and should change about your beliefs and how you're manifesting your reality. Your life will transform into a classroom, where you'll receive a reality-changing curriculum 100 percent personalized to you.

At this access point, a Learn, Grow, Change focus allows you to learn from your reality and the feelings it elicits. What do your reality, and the feelings it gives you, tell you about what you must believe about yourself and your life? Next, this focus directs you to grow your beliefs in accordance with what you've learned. Finally, a Learn, Grow, Change naturally causes your reality, and your experience of it, to change in lockstep with your growth.

Systems Can Change Their Reality

This powerful approach to changing your reality adheres to the nature of systems. When a system changes, it changes its environment. Your self is a system, and when you change it, you also change your environment or reality. A Learn, Grow, Change manifesting focus positions you to change reality in this way.

There are times when you should focus on changing your environment first. Sometimes you should do it immediately, like when you or your loved ones are in danger. From changing your diet to setting boundaries to moving to another city for a job opportunity, there are many occasions when changing your life by changing your environment might be in your best interests.

In the most important parts of your life, however, you should utilize a Learn, Grow, Change focus whenever things become unfulfilling (after accounting for safety and well-being). This gives you the best chance of manifesting and engaging with versions of reality as you truly desire in two important ways.

First, changing your self is something you're always in control of and can do. Yes, there are times when doing that is challenging, but you can still always give your best effort. Even though circumstances can impact your willingness and the effectiveness of your efforts, you are forever seated in the captain's chair.

Second, changing reality through your self allows you to be the source of those changes. Although there are no guarantees for how things will unfold, being the point of origin fosters the greatest potential for positive changes. Intentional manifesting can and will alter your life, so it's in your best interests to be its fountainhead.

What's Ahead?

In this chapter, you'll learn how to access your subconscious and change how you manifest your reality. You'll learn how to grow your incapable beliefs into alignment with your desires. And in so doing, you'll change the form, function, meaning, and value of your reality.

You have no choice about whether or not you manifest your own unique reality. Your only choice is *how* you manifest it. Isn't it wonderful, though, that you can change how you're manifesting, that you have a voice here?

Intentional manifesting does not guarantee that your life will be exactly as you desire. While that is a wonderful outcome, achieving the exact reality you desire isn't the primary focus. Rather, intentional manifesting is all about giving your best effort. And with patience and persistence, it guarantees you can get as close to your most desired versions of reality as possible.

Intentional Manifesting Is for Painful Areas of Your Life

Because it requires effort and time, intentional manifesting is for areas of your life that are painful enough that you're willing to change them. You're ready to bring forth versions of reality that better support your engagement.

Intentional manifesting involves a shift away from *"Where is the version of reality I desire?"* and toward *"How can I manifest this version of reality differently?"* It shifts you away from taking responsibility for your pain and toward taking responsibility for your fulfillment. When life becomes painful, it helps you focus on giving your best effort to change it.

Intentional manifesting is especially helpful when you don't think you need it. When you're certain there's nothing more you can do, when the problems creating your dissatisfaction seem unfixable, you'll be happily surprised by how well it works. The greater the pain, the deeper the impact, and the faster you'll see results.

Access Point Number One: Grow Incapable Beliefs into Alignment with Your Desires

The Main Things to Know About Growing Incapable Beliefs into Alignment with Your Desires:

- **Your beliefs manifest your version of reality.**

- **To change painful versions of reality, you must grow incapable beliefs into alignment with your desires.**

- **To grow incapable beliefs into alignment with your desires, you must communicate with emotional honesty.**

We begin our explanation of intentional manifesting and engagement with access point number one—where you manifest your reality. Your beliefs set the stage for your performances in each moment. And no one has talent great enough to consistently give a world-class performance of *Hamlet* on a stage set for *The Music Man*.

Manifesting the version of reality you desire, one that sets the stage properly for your intended performances, is an imperative. Fortunately, when that is not happening, when your beliefs are incapable, you can change your life by changing your default manifesting settings.

Changing your default manifesting settings is a three-step process:

1. Identify your starting emotional perspective by writing about your painful feelings.

2. Write your way into your new target emotional perspective.

3. Manifest your way into your new target emotional perspective.

In any problematic part of your life, simply repeat those steps until your beliefs are aligned with your desires. In this chapter, I'll walk you through that process.

For performances to have their desired effect, they must be given on a stage set up to fully support them. In fact, the more important your desires, the more essential this is. Versions of reality incapable of supporting your best performances eventually turn you into an Olympic sprinter who's trying to run their race on an ice rink.

A skilled performer can improvise, be quick on their feet, and make clever use of the wrong setup if they're forced to. But that's not a strategy for long-term success and would quickly result in the stage manager getting fired. Don't worry though, you won't be "firing" your beliefs; rather, you'll be helping them grow.

When your life is painful, you're encountering evidence of incapable beliefs. You are not responsible for having these beliefs, but you are responsible for changing them. Unsupportive and unfulfilling versions of reality can and should be put through this belief-raising process.

Most of those beliefs you inherited as a child are still in your subconscious. They are below your conscious awareness though, so you can't see or hear them. But you know they're there by their evidence—the reality they manifest. And you know when your beliefs are incapable by the painful shadows they cast, by the painful feelings they elicit.

Your Subconscious Doesn't Mind If You're Happy

If your subconscious could talk, it would affirm no preference between capable or incapable beliefs. It would tell you that it didn't care whether the beliefs you inherited made you happy, only that they manifested your reality predictably. That's because your subconscious' job isn't to keep you delighted; its job is to keep your self alive. And it will *never* sacrifice predictability, even if the changes would bring you joy.

Your subconscious keeps your beliefs intact because it only speaks the language of emotional honesty. The only way you can communicate with your subconscious and change your beliefs is to use your real feelings. And since your real feelings about painful parts of your life will never be positive, it might appear as though you have no agency here.

Fortunately, your subconscious uses a low-wall security system. Its walls are high enough to keep out all word-based communication and manufactured feelings, but it's also low enough so that your real feelings can still get in. And fortunately, your subconscious is actually fine with you growing your beliefs and manifesting more pleasing versions of reality, as long as your safety is retained every step of the way.

Coach Your Subconscious like a Wild Bunny

Imagine training a wild bunny to eat bread out of your hand. Your subconscious is that wild bunny, and new, aligned beliefs are the bread. You grow your beliefs just like you'd get the bunny closer to your hand—one small, incremental step at a time.

The only way you'd get the bunny to come to your hand would be to lay pieces of bread on the ground closer and closer to you each day. As long as the bunny felt safe, it would inch a little closer to you each day and eat the bread.

Note that the bunny would actually be completely safe at every move forward. In fact, it could've safely walked right up to your hand on the first day and eaten the bread. But since the bunny isn't capable of understanding that, it's your job to lead it forward in a way that works for it. As long as you have patience, that bunny will eventually reach your hand.

Don't worry, your subconscious won't take nearly as long as a wild bunny. Because this process evokes complete emotional honesty, you'll quickly establish rapport with it. This process will build trust faster and more thoroughly than is possible with a wild bunny.

How long will it take to grow incapable beliefs into full alignment? That all depends on where you begin. Usually, the greater the divide between your beliefs and desires, the longer it takes. Greg has found it usually takes him about a month of working this process to bring incapable beliefs into alignment. But bear in mind that the less capable your beliefs are, the more pleasing the new reality they manifest will be.

Use This Process Liberally

Use this process in an area of your life that is painful and important enough that you're willing to do something about it. This will often be a part of your life you've previously tried to change but were unable to achieve the desired effect. Given the limitations of default manifesting, it's perfectly reasonable to employ a low pain threshold here.

Follow the instructions below. With a commitment to radical self-honesty, giving your best, and persistence, your beliefs will grow. In fact, although not yet in line with your true desires, you'll manifest different versions of reality right from the start. That's because your life automatically changes when your beliefs do, just as changing any system automatically changes its environment.

To work this process, you need the Emotional Reference Chart that Greg made for you. It's provided in Chapter Four, but you can also print a copy by visiting this webpage: https://manifestthebigstuff.com/ERC/

The Belief-Raising Process Step One: Identify Your Starting Emotional Perspective by Writing about Your Painful Feelings

Choose a Painful Part of Your Reality

Choose one important desire that's painfully absent from your life. Choose only one—use this process on one desire at a time so as not to dilute your focus or its power. Pick one aspect of your life that causes sorrow—something you've tried to change but with little to no success. One that is important enough that you're willing to put in the effort to change it.

Greg has used this belief-raising process to get out of debt, find a soulmate, build a business, and write a book. Just as he did, you should select something essential to your success and fulfillment. You might use this process on an important part of your life, like being healthy, losing weight, making money, parenting your child, succeeding at work, or another that has been a little too painful for you.

Emotional pain serves as the feedback about the distance between your beliefs' capabilities and the versions of reality you truly desire. Follow that feedback. It's a shadow cast by incapable beliefs. And don't fret too much about which desire to use this process on because you can do this process again and again.

Get To Your True Feelings by Writing about Them

Once you've selected a painfully absent desire, keep it and mind while asking yourself these questions (filling in the blank with your specific desire): *"How do I really feel about the absence of (this desire)? How does the absence of (this desire) really make me feel about myself, my worth, my value, and what others think of me?"* Then, declare your desire aloud in a proactive statement, as if you currently possess and experience it, and pay close attention to how you feel about its absence.

For example, if you want to use this process to improve your painfully limited finances, state, *"I am as wealthy as I desire. I have all the money I need and I have no money worries."* Then start writing down all the unpleasant feelings that statement elicits.

As an aside, sometimes your pain involves the presence of something unwanted rather than the absence of something desired. You might have a ton of debt, for example, and need to rid yourself of it. When that's the case, focus on what you want to replace the unwanted thing with. When Greg used this process for the first time to get rid of his debt, he phrased his desire as *"I have all the money I need to pay my debts and keep my family's finances healthy."*

Be reflective and soul-searching. First responses may not be as honest as you can be, so keep digging. Avoid writing intentionally positive thoughts about how you wish you felt about it and ignore how you "ought" to feel about it. Bypass ways you've previously justified or rationalized this desire's absence in your life. Meet the pain head-on, with radical self-honesty, and write it all down.

Write in free form. Let your painful thoughts and feelings flow onto the page without analyzing or judging them. This may be an unpleasant subject to write about and may feel like emotional vomit. But be radically self-honest, no matter how painful it is. Put it all out there on paper, warts and all. Write without worrying about how you "should" feel or how somebody might judge you.

Be Radically Self-Honest

To effectively use this process and grow your beliefs, you must get honest about how you really feel, right now. Your subconscious brain is physically constructed, after all, so it can neither hear nor adopt better feelings than what's already there. The pain you're writing about comes from the divide between what your beliefs are capable of manifesting and what your desires for life are. When that divide gets big enough, it can feel like a wound—jump into that cut.

As an added benefit, when you write in free-form, when you lose yourself in the free, unedited flow of thoughts and words, you and I are able to communicate directly. Writing in free-form allows me to help you write candidly about your feelings and what they mean to you. Lose yourself completely, and you might even watch, like a spectator, as your pen moves across the page as if it has a life of its own.

Keep your writing completely private because you're writing for yourself alone. Provide the privacy you need to write with courage and tenacity; do not hold back. Be radically self-honest; describe how you truly feel about the painful absence of this desire. You can always burn your writings when you're through with them.

Writing about These Feelings Won't Make Them Real

You'll be writing about feelings like anxiety, grief, worthlessness, dejection, and hopelessness. Whatever comes out is what's inside of you. You won't create those feelings by writing about them, nor will you breathe more life into them, because what comes out is already very real inside you. You are merely acknowledging the shadows of incapable beliefs.

Every human inherits some incapable beliefs, so what other kind of shadows would you expect? You wouldn't be attempting to grow new beliefs if they were already capable. There is nothing you can do about having incapable beliefs as an adult except to grow new ones now. And to grow beliefs into alignment, you must start from where you really are.

Your job with this initial writing session is not to elevate your perspective or find a way to see this problem in a way that makes you feel better about it right now. Don't attempt to write yourself up, if you will, into a more positive viewpoint. You're not out to make yourself feel worse than you already do, but it's important to keep this writing focused on your most applicable, relevant <u>painful</u> feelings.

Find Your Starting Point on the Emotional Reference Chart

Write, write, and write until you feel you've emptied your gut of all the negative, scary, bad-feeling stuff in there. Don't try to put things into a perspective that eases the discomfort; rather, just put all your raw thoughts and emotions out there. Then use the major themes found in your writing and your intuition to identify where on the Emotional Reference Chart you are starting from. As you can see, the Emotional Reference Chart is a list of ascending emotional perspectives. Find the emotional perspective on the chart that matches your current feelings about your painfully absent desire. If it helps, use a dictionary to look up definitions (you'll be using one in Step Two anyway).

The differences between emotional perspectives on the chart are subtle, by design. If you feel uncertain about which one fits your writing the best, a simple solution is to choose the lowest perspective from the group you're considering. There's no reason to worry about starting too low because you'll be heading in the same direction, up, no matter where you start.

Greg's Emotional Reference Chart (From Chapter Four)

1. Love/Ecstasy

2. Joy/Elation

3. Ease/Power

4. Confidence/Inspiration

5. Excitement/Passion

6. Anticipation/Eagerness

7. Enthusiasm/Ambition

8. Hopefulness/Optimism

9. Interest/Inquisitiveness

10. Acceptance/Peace

11. Introspection/Contemplation

12. Pensiveness/Melancholy

13. Indifference/Apathy

14. Unease/Discontent

15. Frustration/Aggravation

16. Worry/Nervousness

17. Doubt/Pessimism

18. Anger/Blame

19. Anxiety/Fear

20. Grief/Desolation

21. Despair/Worthlessness

22. Powerlessness/Dejection

23. Depression/Hopelessness

When you find the best match for what you wrote, that emotional perspective becomes your starting point. Your true painful feelings about this part of your life are where you begin the next part of this process. Don't worry though, there is no starting point on the chart that is too low for you to use it successfully.

The Belief-Raising Process Step Two: Write Your Way into Your New Target Emotional Perspective

On the Emotional Reference Chart, find the next highest emotional perspective. For example, if you just wrote about Grief/Desolation, you will look to Anxiety/Fear. Anxiety/Fear will be your new target emotional perspective.

Write about Your Absent Desire from This New Target Perspective

Write down the names of the new target emotions and look up their definitions to ensure you understand them. Then answer the question: *"What must I believe about myself and my life in this part of reality to feel this way about not having (my desire)?"* If, for example, your new target emotional perspective is Anxiety/Fear, ask yourself, *"What must I believe about myself and my life in this part of reality to feel anxiety and fear about (my desire) being absent?"*

You can also try, *"How would this part of reality need to work for me to feel anxiety and fear about (my desire) being absent?"* and *"What would it mean about my worth, value, and what others think about me in this part of reality to feel anxiety and fear about (my desire) being absent?"*

Use the definitions of the new target emotions as prompts to guide your writing and frame your answers to those questions. As before, write in free-form, letting your thoughts and feelings flow onto the page without analyzing or judging them. Again, be radically self-honest, no matter how painful. As always, this writing is for you alone, and complete emotional honesty is the key to accessing your subconscious.

You never know what your writing will reveal about how you can see and understand this part of your life differently in ways that fit your new target perspective. But rest assured, as you continue the process, you will be slightly empowered by it. The new reality you write about will involve a bit more proactivity from you in manifesting your solutions.

Your free-form writing will uncover ways to see and understand a slightly more aligned reality, one that will elicit the feelings of your new target emotional perspective. That new reality may not even be what you would traditionally call "positive" for a while yet, but that's okay. Continue to be radically self-honest and embrace the incremental improvements, knowing that's the pace your subconscious needs to feel safe.

The New Perspective Is Hardly More Aligned than Your Previous One

Step Two makes one thing immediately apparent—there's hardly any improvement between emotional perspectives on the chart. That is intentional. Because each new emotional perspective offers little improvement over the one before it, you're prevented from taking a quantum leap of positivity. This means your subconscious will go along for the ride each time you move up one emotional perspective.

The slight improvements allow you to communicate with your subconscious because you're speaking its native tongue of emotional honesty. It recognizes that the new emotional perspective is basically the same as the previous one. Or at least it understands that any improvement is too small to be threatened by it. Thus, you are able to lead your subconscious to grow your beliefs slightly more into alignment with your desires with each step up the Emotional Reference Chart.

If your subconscious could talk, it would say, *"These new feelings we're writing about? They're honest; they match up with how we really feel. They're safe. I will listen to them and adopt them. It's safe for me to allow our beliefs to grow this small amount."* To your subconscious, the new target emotional perspective is basically the same as the one that preceded it. Your subconscious hears and adopts the new target emotional perspective, and just like that, your beliefs have actually become just a little bit more aligned.

The Slight Growth in Alignment Is Intentional

Just like that bunny you trained, your subconscious isn't bothered that your life is a little more pleasing because it's still just as predictable. You're teaching it that this slightly more aligned new emotional perspective still keeps you safe.

Speak its language of emotional honesty, and your subconscious will gladly follow, one baby step of improvement at a time. Your subconscious doesn't care that your new emotional perspective is a little more aligned with your desires because it's not a quantum leap of positivity. And your life *is* still genuinely just as predictable as before; you're not fooling your subconscious—you're leading it.

The minor improvements are the key to this process. Even though each improvement is small, each *is* an actual improvement. The reality your new emotional perspective manifests <u>is</u> slightly more aligned with your desires. Each new emotional perspective empowers you in slight but noticeable ways and sometimes in ways you wouldn't have guessed.

New target emotional perspectives, which at first glance appear to offer little to no improvement, actually do. Unexpected solutions come out of your pen as you write in free form. Who knew, for example, that feeling anxiety/fear about this part of your life could offer more opportunities than desolation? Your writing will reveal hidden opportunities every time.

The Belief-Raising Process Step Three: Manifest Your Way into Your New Target Emotional Perspective

Now you get to start manifesting this part of your reality from the new emotional perspective you just wrote about. Use your writing to help you see and understand it differently. Allow your new emotional perspective to be reflected back to you by this part of your life as you live your way into it.

Manifest This Area of Your Life from Your New Perspective

Let the new emotional perspective serve as a filter through which you now see this part of your life. Consider your chosen desire from the perspective of the writing you just did. Think about it and let it ruminate. Imagine yourself as an actor and the writing you just did as a new script. How would you play your role differently now? How would you act out this part differently, and how would that change the whole production?

You wrote about it; now you get to bring it to life.

This step is where your life actually changes. It may not yet be at the level you truly desire, but the changes will be real and noticeable. You will now watch this part of your life transform right in front of your eyes. Familiar people, places, and things take on new meaning and value, if not new form and function, reflecting these new beliefs. Your problems and challenges start to reveal previously hidden opportunities.

Allow your writing from Step Two to inspire how you see and understand your reality differently. That writing has stimulated new actions, ideas, attitudes, and focus, and now you get to follow through on them. Be patient rather than demanding with your new reality, keeping in mind that these aren't grand changes you're manifesting. Keep appropriate expectations of incremental growth, and your new emotional perspective will, of its own accord, manifest new versions of reality.

Reassure Your Subconscious

The minor improvements to your life will ease any concerns your subconscious might have. But if you're struggling with the new perspective for any reason, assure your subconscious:

"I understand any hesitancy to manifest this part of our reality from this emotional perspective, because our old perspectives are very familiar. Yet we are perfectly safe to manifest it from this new perspective because it is basically no more positive than the previous one. There truly is no reason for us to be scared of it. This new perspective is believable, safe, and okay to adopt."

Because you'll be telling your subconscious the truth, it usually shouldn't need much more coaxing beyond that. These won't be large or wholesale improvements, after all, so it's not a heavy lift. It won't feel like too much of a stretch to manifest this part of your life in these new ways. Because your new emotions are close enough to what's already there, your subconscious listens and allows your beliefs to grow in response.

Your new version of reality will be slightly more aligned with your desires for it. Although not how you want to ultimately manifest it, of course, the improvements will be obvious enough to notice at each new emotional perspective. These will be changes in how you see and understand this part of your life, and they will often sound elementary to an outside observer.

For example, when moving to Worry/Nervousness, you might see and understand that you're worried about never having what you desire in this part of your life. That's not a positive emotional state and it's not something that someone will congratulate you for. But being worried about whether or not your desire manifests is a big (yet subtle) experiential step in the right direction compared to the state of Doubt/Pessimism which preceded it.

And don't worry—your subconscious won't be spooked by you noticing the improvements because it knows the changes are safe. Even as you enter the positive emotional perspectives and the changes are more obviously aligned with your desired outcomes, you'll have arrived from emotions only slightly less so. So each step forms a gradual, natural, and believable upward progress.

The Slight Improvements Will Get You There

You will sometimes be tempted by the familiarity of emotions lower on the chart. It's normal for your subconscious to prefer familiar pain over unfamiliar joy. And sometimes you'll want to look ahead and imagine life from a higher emotional perspective. Whenever that happens, gently remind yourself to return to your current emotional perspective and reframe things from there.

There are undoubtedly parts of your life where you could authentically raise your emotional perspective more than one step up the chart during one writing session. However, for areas painful enough to use this process on, always resist that temptation. Not because it's an impossible feat here, but because you will always cheat yourself out of the learning, growth, and change that would've occurred during your time spent with each emotional perspective you skipped over.

Even when you can jump ahead, don't, because you don't want to miss any of the individualized curriculum I have for you. If you ever find you truly don't need to work your way up the Emotional Reference Chart so deliberately, congratulations! This most likely means you simply chose an issue minor enough that you didn't need this formal belief-raising process.

Repeat the writing and living cycle each day until you've manifested this part of your life as you wish it to be. Because you're not making a quantum leap, it usually takes one to three days to manifest this part of your life from the new perspective. But if you're not manifesting this part of your reality like that after day three, who cares? Keep doing this for as long as you need.

You'll never manifest from Love/Ecstasy without manifesting your reality from where you are right now. So each time you complete Step Three of this process, congratulate yourself. You've just completed the most important part of this entire process—the one you're currently on!

Repeat Steps Two and Three with each perspective on the Emotional Reference Chart until you reach the top. Each improvement up the chart is like setting the piece of bread a little closer to you. All your subconscious cares about is the safety of your new, slightly more aligned reality; it is not concerned that it's more pleasing.

As soon as your life reflects the slight alignment of your new target emotional perspective, you've really done it—you've grown your beliefs. Maybe not as much as you ultimately want to grow them yet, but each minor improvement is actually the most important step.

One emotional perspective at a time, retain your commitment to radical self-honesty and persistence. Be tenacious; don't let life's ups and downs stop you. Keep applying yourself to this process, no matter what, and you will keep discovering opportunities to manifest your desire differently.

Your Journey to the Top of the Emotional Reference Chart

Depending on your starting point, it usually takes Greg about a month to reach the top of the Emotional Reference Chart. But you don't have to be at the top before you start manifesting better versions of reality. Your life improves from your first move up the chart, and seeing that change, in real time, is exciting and motivating.

You began this process by stating your desire aloud, as if you were already manifesting it. Each step of this journey changed you. You adopted new emotional perspectives that nudged your beliefs a bit more into alignment with your desires each time. And as you change, so does your reality; your outer world always changes to reflect changes to your inner world.

Even if your reality isn't radically altered in form, its function, meaning, and value are transformed in accordance with you. For example, the cheating spouse that prompted you to use this process might still be someone you need to divorce. But you now see and understand yourself differently enough to have healthier boundaries, trust your instincts more, and be unafraid to call out someone's bad behavior and hold them accountable for it. You will manifest romance (and many other parts of your life) in new ways, from this moment forward, because this is authentically who you are now.

You are coaching your subconscious, growing out of incapable beliefs given to you during childhood, using a Learn, Grow, Change manifesting focus. You're forward-scripting reality with this process. You're identifying the feeling perspective of a new version of reality, slightly improved from a previous one, and then using those feelings to live your way into it.

There is no need to figure out how your desired version of reality will eventually manifest. When you arrive at the top of the chart, life often shows up differently than you might've imagined. That's because you can only see that life, and all the new opportunities it provides, from those higher perspectives.

Keep It to One Step at a Time

It is very important to only move up one emotion at a time. Feeling snippets of higher emotions about this aspect of your life is natural. You have plenty of capable beliefs too, so envisioning better versions of reality is normal. Don't worry about feeling emotions better than your current perspective; just refocus on what you've written.

Alternatively, you don't need to also manifest other parts of your life from the lower parts of the chart. You should continue to feel great about aspects of your life that are pleasing to you. That's authentic, also matches what's already in your subconscious, and won't prevent growing your incapable beliefs into alignment.

When emotions lower on the chart re-emerge during this process, a good practice is to make sure you're not too hungry, angry, lonely, tired, or serious. Get something to eat, blow off some steam, talk with a friend, get some rest, or find a moment to gently laugh with yourself. And assure your subconscious with soothing talk such as:

"That's an old belief, and I understand why you went there—it's familiar. But we have authentically moved up the Emotional Reference Chart and actually have new beliefs now. Although I understand where that perspective comes from, it's perfectly okay to focus on the new ones we have genuinely embraced and accepted."

Your subconscious won't understand your words, of course. But it'll certainly appreciate and connect with the authentic emotional perspectives you're conveying.

The Growth Is Deliberate but Steady

Don't fret about the seemingly slow pace of the process. Do not get in a rush and try to shortcut it. Remember that your subconscious needs to keep being coaxed into alignment with new beliefs—especially on the higher end of the Emotional Reference Chart.

Moving too quickly can elicit scary, out-of-control feelings such as impending doom. If that happens, simply slow down, backtrack as much as needed, and spend a little more time with the previous emotional perspective. Put your attention and focus back on the previous emotional perspective and remind yourself that the step you're on is the most important one in this process.

For example, you might be so excited by the next emotional perspective of Confidence/Inspiration that you rush into it. Your enthusiasm is understandable since you're transforming such a painfully unsatisfying part of your life. After where you started, who wouldn't be eager?

If you find yourself feeling worried about how the changes you really want will come about, because you still can't see how that could be possible right now, you might take a step back. Trying to figure out how your desires will manifest, rather than letting your beliefs change your life naturally, of their own accord, is a red-light indicator to slow down. Feeling nervous, anxious, worried, or uncertain are all signs that you might've needed more time at the previous perspective before moving on.

There is no need to rush. Take your time because you, literally, aren't in charge of manufacturing your new reality. All you need to do is adopt your current emotional perspective, and your subconscious will take care of the changes for you.

Greg has experienced his life being noticeably more aligned with his desires somewhere around emotional perspective number eight: Hopefulness/Optimism. At that point, he has grown his incapable beliefs into alignment with traditionally positive emotions. But keep writing and manifesting, and you will continue to see and understand even better versions of reality.

Higher Emotional Perspectives Are Challenging in Their Own Way

Don't be surprised if arriving at positive emotions on the chart proves unexpectedly challenging. You've grown quite accustomed to the painful life created by your incapable beliefs. Those incapable beliefs may have been painful, but there has been a measure of comfort in their familiarity.

Beliefs now grown into greater alignment can cultivate opportunities where previously there were mostly problems. Producing better versions of life doesn't mean issues no longer exist; it means your new beliefs can manifest the opportunities inherent in them more readily. The problems don't go away; they're just not all you see anymore.

The best opportunities arise from the biggest problems, which is why they can feel overwhelming sometimes. The bigger the problem you're solving, the greater the opportunities it provides. And after so much frustration and pain, it may take some time to get used to seeing opportunities in this area of your life.

Reaching the Top of the Chart Extends Your Journey

Being at Love/Ecstasy will manifest a version of reality matching that perspective. With effort and persistence, you will eventually manifest the form, function, meaning, and value of this part of your life from it. Your new beliefs will create a version of reality that provide opportunities and inspiration in line with this new alignment.

You never have to finish this journey either, as even grander desires will always emerge from your fulfillment. In fact, if you're invested in life and giving your best, expect to regularly encounter new desires that your beliefs cannot manifest. That's good news—it means you're dreaming bigger and seeing even more potential for success. You can now grow your beliefs into alignment with grander desires as often as you want and need.

You came to this earthly world for the opportunity to intentionally manifest life, to take this journey. You didn't come to play small or pretend you are unimportant; you came to give your best effort to intentionally manifest important parts of your life the way you really want them to be. Giving your best effort to change a painful part of your life is that journey.

CHAPTER SIX

HOW TO INTENTIONALLY ENGAGE WITH YOUR REALITY

The Main Thing to Know About Intentionally Engaging with Your Reality:

- **To intentionally engage with your reality, do two things:**

1. Align yourself each morning with the opportunities that are presented to you in each moment.

2. Use techniques that guide you through a "Learn, Grow, Change" manifesting focus.

Anytime your reality is unfulfilling or painful, you can and should engage with it more intentionally. You can utilize two distinct access points to change your default engagement settings. At these two points you can:

- Access your conscious mind to change how you prepare to engage with your reality.

- Again access your conscious mind to change how you engage with your reality.

As with the first access point in the previous chapter, these two can also be referred to as "pinch points" since they are where much of life's distress is created when default settings fail to deliver the desired outcomes. When life is unsatisfying, that pain is a signal that your approach to reality is inadequate. This section will teach you how to address insufficient engagement with reality.

The most effective strategy for each pinch point is to apply a Learn, Grow, Change approach to your engagement. You will learn how to identify what you can and should alter about your approach to reality. Your life will become a classroom where you receive a curriculum for changing reality that is 100 percent customized to you.

At this access point, a Learn, Grow, Change focus allows you to learn from your reality and the feelings it elicits. What does your reality, and the feelings it gives you, tell you about how you're engaging with it? Next, this focus directs you to grow your ways of engaging with reality in accordance with what you've learned. Finally, Learn, Grow, Change naturally causes your reality and your experience of it to change in lockstep with your growth.

Systems Can Change Their Reality

This potent method of transforming your reality aligns with the principles of systems. As a system changes, it modifies its surroundings. As an individual, you are a system, and when you modify yourself, you also alter your environment or reality. Embracing a Learn, Grow, Change manifesting approach empowers you to change reality in this manner.

There are circumstances when it is essential to concentrate on changing your environment first. For instance, in a situation where your safety or the safety of someone you're responsible for is in danger, you should first alter your circumstances. There are various occasions, from changing your eating habits to relocating to a new city for work, when changing your life by changing your environment may be in your best interest.

However, in the most crucial aspects of your life, you should adopt a Learn, Grow, Change approach when things become unsatisfactory (after ensuring safety and well-being). This provides you with the best opportunity to interact with the versions of reality that you genuinely desire in two crucial ways.

Firstly, modifying yourself is a task that you always have control over and can accomplish. Even though there may be moments when it's difficult, you can still give it your all. While circumstances may impact your willingness and effectiveness, you are always in charge.

Secondly, changing reality by transforming yourself allows you to be the originator of those changes. Although there are no assurances regarding how things will proceed, being the starting point fosters the highest potential for positive changes. Intentionally manifesting can and will transform your life, so it is in your best interest to be the fountainhead of that change.

What's Ahead?

In this chapter you're going to learn how to access your conscious mind and change how you prepare to engage with your reality. You'll learn how to set yourself up to take advantage of the opportunities provided to you in each moment of the day. Doing this will give you the best chance to successfully engage with your reality.

Then you'll learn how to access your conscious mind again and change how you engage with your reality. You'll learn how to apply a Learn, Grow, Change manifesting focus to default engagement that just isn't working. This will allow you the greatest influence over creating more successful engagements with reality.

Every Human Manifests and Engages with Reality

You cannot opt out of engaging with your reality. Your only decision is *how* you'll engage. And isn't it cool that you have choices here and the ability to do it more intentionally?

Intentional engagement doesn't promise an exact match to your desired reality. Though achieving precisely what you wish is amazing, it's not the main goal. The primary focus of intentional engagement is to give your best effort, and with perseverance and consistency, it guarantees that you'll get as close as possible to your desired experiences of reality.

Intentional Engagement Is for Painful Areas of Your Life

Intentional engagement is a commitment to change the areas of your life that cause enough pain to motivate you. It requires dedicating time and effort to experiencing versions of reality that better align with your goals. To achieve this, you need to prepare yourself daily and stay focused on your efforts.

The shift from *"Why is this happening to me?"* to *"How can I engage with this reality differently?"* is crucial in intentional engagement. It changes your perspective from blaming external factors to taking responsibility for your own fulfillment. By focusing on giving your best effort, you can transform your painful experiences.

Intentional engagement can be particularly useful when you don't think you need it. Even when you believe your problems are unsolvable, intentional engagement can yield surprisingly positive results. The more painful the situation, the greater the impact of intentional engagement, and the faster you'll see results.

Access Point Number Two: Vibrationally Align Yourself with Your Opportunities

The Main Things to Know About Vibrationally Aligning Yourself with Your Opportunities:

- **Vibrationally aligning yourself is a daily practice.**

- **Starting your day with this practice prepares you to deliver the best performances possible.**

- **You can align yourself with your opportunities no matter your circumstances.**

We continue our exploration of intentional engagement with access point number two, how you prepare yourself to engage with reality. Aligning yourself vibrationally with your opportunities to perform is the most powerful and important way to begin each day. Doing this increases your chances of delivering your best performances and engaging successfully.

Each moment of your life is an opportunity to manifest reality and engage with it. In fact, this moment is the only place you'll ever be alive, so it's the only one where you will ever do that.

Each moment is given to you with no strings attached. Once they're gone, they're gone. But as long as you're still alive, more are given to you. As precious as they are, you do not have to earn them, nor will you be punished for not taking full advantage of them.

Being properly prepared to take advantage of each moment's unparalleled opportunities creates your greatest chances to give world-class performances. But even giving your best effort on a stage set to perfectly support you cannot overcome being unprepared. It takes vibrational alignment to consistently spot and take advantage of what you're offered in each moment.

Each Morning, Write Your Way into Vibrational Alignment with Your Opportunities

Begin your morning by journaling, in free form, about the opportunities that await you in every moment of the day ahead. Writing in free-form means you let your thoughts and words flow onto the paper without editing or censoring. Writing this way opens up a clear channel between us and allows me to communicate with you directly. Your journaling doesn't need to be a certain length—simply keep writing until you're vibrationally aligned enough to give your best effort to take advantage of each moment. And don't worry about how it might sound to anyone else—this writing is for you alone.

Let's take a moment to differentiate this journaling from the writing you do during the belief-raising process. This journaling is a daily process, designed to acclimate you to the day ahead, rather than writing focused on making incremental improvements to a specific desire you wish to manifest. Additionally, this journaling is a preparatory exercise done each morning, as opposed to the belief-raising process, which has a beginning and end.

Write about how, in each moment, you get to be fully present and alive, able to give your best effort to intentionally manifest your life and engage with it. Each moment is your opportunity to choose your actions, ideas, attitudes, and focus and then follow through on them. Aligning yourself vibrationally is a daily practice, done every morning before setting out into the world.

Journal to align yourself with your opportunities, not the specific outcomes you want. Journal about how priceless every moment is, how each is a onetime event, never to return. Having access to it only once makes it an incredibly valuable commodity. Allow each moment's significance to motivate you to take full advantage of it.

Journal about how special it is to be able to give your best effort. In life, all you can ask for is an opportunity, and when you get one, all you can do is your best. Today, you're getting a lot of opportunities, and you have the option of giving your best effort during every one of them.

Align Yourself with Opportunities, Not Outcomes

Taking advantage of your opportunities doesn't mean you will always have your nose to the grindstone and work, work, work. You're going to have downtime; you'll scroll through social media and do other "nonproductive" things. But vibrational alignment means you'll be prepared to roll up your sleeves when you choose to.

If you are excited to jump into the day with gusto, so be it, but that isn't the goal of your journaling. Vibrational alignment doesn't require you to get amped up about the day, just aligned with its opportunities. Your goal is to be prepared to take full advantage of any moment you choose.

Here is an example of vibrational alignment from Greg Kuhn's journal:

6/13

June! Sun is up. I am up.

Day is here, moments are here, opportunities are here. No strings attached. Didn't ask for them—they're simply given to me.

I can waste them if I choose. Hide under my covers all day long. No punishment for those choices, just missed opportunities is all. I don't want to do that—just giving the example.

What do I want to do today? Take advantage of these opportunities to the best of my ability! To be a tremendous ally to my future self (and my present self as I cultivate and experience joy)! To be fully present and alive, right now in this moment (and the moments to come), so that I can best and most intentionally manifest my reality. A version of reality as closely aligned with my desires as possible.

Today. All day to the best of my ability. Let's do this.

You can see that Greg didn't write himself into alignment with any specific outcomes, nor even with *successfully* manifesting and engaging with his life. Rather, he aligned himself with his opportunities to do those things. And a lengthy writing session wasn't required either. He only wrote as much as necessary to achieve that alignment.

You'll Be Performing Today, No Matter How Your Stage is Set

You're going to perform in each moment today, whether or not the stage is set supportively. So regardless of the capability of your beliefs to manifest reality, it's imperative you align yourself with the performances you're able to deliver in each moment. Such alignment creates your best chance of recognizing opportunities and taking advantage of them.

Taking advantage of an opportunity creates the highest potential that you'll be pleased and fulfilled. Giving your best effort to manifest life as you truly desire is your most reliable way to consistently do that. And this moment is that opportunity.

You're not aligning yourself with the outcomes of your efforts but rather with your opportunities to manifest them. This is a very important distinction because your circumstances will vary and sometimes prove more challenging, but opportunities will always be there.

Align Yourself with Your Opportunities Whether You Feel Good about Them or Not

One of the best things about vibrationally aligning yourself is that you can do it under any circumstances. You can be aligned with opportunities without feeling good about them.

Even amid the worst circumstances, when you're certain the opportunities will be scarce or of poor quality, you can align yourself with them if you're willing.

Vibrational alignment journaling is not a pep talk—you're not pumping yourself up. You're synching up with the opportunities in each moment to choose your actions, ideas, attitudes, and focus and follow through on them. No matter how you feel about your self or your current version of reality, you can align yourself with what each moment provides.

Here is an example of vibrational alignment from Greg Kuhn's journal on a day he did not feel good about his life:

9/23

I'm feeling discouraged by my "student" status today. By my PC, my lack of access to a fast workflow, from not knowing what the hell I'm doing, and my hardware. It's making me feel like I am a fraud—that I don't really have any ideas of value. That I'm fooling myself.

It sucks. This is where I am.

All the work I've done since last January and it's basically worthless. I still don't have anything to offer for sale. Nothing to make money. And my podcast, at the moment, feels like a big vanity project.

This is where positive affirmations come in. Because everything I just wrote is bullshit. It is how I actually feel this morning, so I am acknowledging it. But it is based on lies.

I have not wasted my time. I do have much to say, share, and teach. People do want to hear what I have to say, share, and teach. And all the work I've done up to this point, any work I've done, is part of my journey. Part of building me, my brand, my message. Part of manifesting my self. Informing my message—fleshing it out. Figuring out what is important and what can go.

Nothing is wasted. Nothing is inconsequential. It all counts for something, even if that something ends up being internally realized. Because there is no difference between internal and external. What's going on in here is also going on out there.

Today offers me the exact same opportunities, in practice and principle, that my most upbeat day does. It's okay not to be pumped up, excited, or jumping for joy today. That doesn't diminish the opportunities I have today. And it doesn't mean I can't, or won't, take great advantage of them either.

Writing creates my joy—it is a source of joy. I don't need to have joy conferred upon me to write. I can do virtually anything today, despite or in spite of any feelings I have. I can and will take advantage of the opportunities given to me today, without strings. Opportunities to be fully present and alive in this moment and others that follow. And intentionally manifest a reality that I desire. And one that will make my future self happy and pleased.

Let's do it. Productive input and productive output—it's not only a simple formula, it's an effective one too. Let's do this.

You can see that Greg didn't give himself a stereotypical, feel-good pep talk designed to get himself excited. Instead, he acknowledged how he actually felt about his life and stated that opportunities were still present despite feeling crappy about it. While his journaling didn't catapult him into some ideal mindset, that's okay. It still put him in the best position possible to take advantage of what was there.

Always Control What's in Your Control

Speaking of crappy versions of life, at the end of the day, many factors outside of your control will influence your life. Therefore, it's always in your best interest, and often imperative, for you to take charge of the things you <u>do</u> have control over. You have too much riding on your engagement with reality in the important areas of your life to simply voluntarily surrender your ability to be prepared to engage.

Experiencing displeasure is simply part of being human. Because of the separation you experience here, you're going to be without things you desire, and you're going to experience loss. When that happens in important parts of your reality, life gets challenging really quickly.

The bigger your desires, the more challenging it becomes to spot opportunities because the problems you're solving are bigger too. This highlights the importance of vibrationally aligning yourself with them each day—it's more difficult to take advantage of opportunities when vibrationally you're feeling threatened, unsafe, worried, or concerned.

Vibrational Alignment Takes Advantage of Correlation

Correlation is a term used to describe nonlocal connections between people, places, and things in material reality. To be correlated with another part of your reality means you can communicate with it, instantly in real time, without being in its presence. Daily vibrational alignment allows you to use the combined power of intention and meditation to correlate with each moment of life.

Daily vibrational alignment creates an intention to take advantage of the opportunity in each moment, and free-form journaling is a form of active meditation. So this technique checks both boxes and allows you to correlate with each moment and the opportunities it gives you. What is life, after all, but a series of moments, a series of stages set for you to perform upon?

You can correlate and then communicate with parts of your reality as if you are one entity, because you actually are. On an energy level, you share consciousness with everything else in your life. Since we are the same energy field, you can correlate with any other person, place, or thing that is also capable of existing in and engaging with reality.

What you're actually correlating here is "present you" and "future you" (who will exist in the next moment and every moment after that). You're communicating with "future you" in real time to share information about taking advantage of opportunities. Should you also seek correlation with the outcomes you want and not just the opportunities to create them? While there is nothing wrong with doing that, it's always best to focus primarily on opportunities because many of the factors influencing outcomes will be out of your control.

Align Yourself, Especially on the Days It Doesn't Come Naturally

Some days you've awakened excited by the day ahead, eager to engage with your reality without journaling about those opportunities. You've taken advantage of opportunities before, despite not having aligned yourself with them. Everyone has had the experience of enthusiasm for life without intentional vibrational alignment.

The importance of this practice, however, is highlighted by all the other days when you're *not* naturally excited by what the day offers. This practice is for Monday mornings, when you wish you didn't have to go to work. It's for the days you're worried about how something important will turn out. It's for the times you feel discouraged, like you've been wasting your time and no good will come from your efforts.

Days and moments like those are frequent and normal. They don't necessarily mean you're doing something wrong, but you don't have to let them dictate whether or not you're fully prepared to perform. A daily practice of aligning yourself with the day's opportunities won't protect you from undesirable circumstances, but it will put you in the best position to give an adequate performance despite them.

Alignment—Don't Start Your Day without It!

Whether you wake up excited about your opportunities or not, start each day by vibrationally aligning yourself with them. Don't stop writing until you're ready to give your best efforts to take advantage of your opportunities, regardless of what life appears to have in store for you today. Do this first thing each morning, and you will be prepared as possible to perform in each moment.

Access Point Number Three: How to Successfully Engage with Your Reality

The Main Thing to Know about Successfully Engaging with Your Reality:

- **The best way to successfully engage with your reality is with a Learn, Grow, Change manifesting focus.**

We wrap up our examination of intentional engagement with access point number three—how you engage with your reality. Your engagement, or performance, is facilitated through your conscious mind, where you sit in the captain's chair and choose your actions, ideas, attitudes, and focus. And just as importantly, engagement is how you follow through with those decisions.

Successful performances are best done by intentionally engaging your reality with a commitment to learn, grow, and change. In the next chapter, you'll find eight reality-engagement techniques steeped in that focus. These techniques will consistently assist you in making great decisions and following through on them.

Because your engagement with life is public-facing, you could call what's awaiting you in the next chapter "performance techniques." Everyone who cares enough to pay attention can see how you're engaging with your life, after all. You can't successfully fake your way through life for long; if you aren't making good decisions and following through on them, people will eventually notice.

These eight techniques you're about to learn help you ditch the status quo by empowering you to use your feelings as information. They help you use your emotions as intended—as feedback about the capability of your beliefs and the adequacy of your engagement. And they prioritize feeling and processing your emotions, so you can learn from them, grow your engagement with reality, and then change your reality from the inside out.

These eight techniques all help you:

- Identify inadequate engagement

- Adapt to adequately engage

- Put it all into action

When important parts of your life become painful, using a Learn, Grow, Change focus is your most reliable way of escaping the confines of inadequate engagement. To make their explanations uniform and help you employ them, each of the eight techniques reveals:

1. When to use the technique

2. How to use the technique

3. Why the technique works

These Learn, Grow, Change manifesting techniques unleash the tremendous power you, as a system, have to change your environment or your life. By changing your self, as a primary method of changing your life, you retain the ability to engage no matter your circumstances. And it's always in your best interests to be the source of that change.

There are definitely times when you should change your environment first, such as when you or someone you love is in danger. Always provide safety first; remove yourself from harmful situations and establish boundaries where needed. After doing that, however, return to these techniques and a focus on self-change. When teamed with aligned beliefs and vibrational alignment, these eight techniques can move mountains.

CHAPTER SEVEN

EIGHT INTENTIONAL ENGAGEMENT TECHNIQUES

The Main Things to Know about these Intentional Engagement Techniques:

- **All eight techniques help you concentrate on a Learn, Grow, Change manifesting focus.**

- **The following techniques help you engage successfully with reality in three ways. They help you:**

1. Make the best decisions about your actions, ideas, attitudes, and focus.

2. Give your best effort to follow through on those decisions.

3. Keep you focused on learning, growing, and changing.

In this chapter, we'll discuss eight techniques that will help you engage with life more intentionally and successfully. Engaging with life is a crucial aspect of fulfillment, but unfortunately, many people get caught up in the daily grind and forget the power they wield as CEO to engage more intentionally with their reality. This leads to feelings of dissatisfaction, disillusionment, and even depression.

Intentionally engaging with reality means being present and fully participating in the experiences that come your way. It involves taking risks, stepping out of your comfort zone, and embracing new challenges. It requires a mindset of growth and a willingness to learn and evolve. These eight techniques are tailor-made to help you do all that and, even more importantly, keep you squarely focused on learning, growing, and changing.

In this chapter, we will explore eight techniques that will help you engage more successfully with life. Each technique is designed to help you overcome common obstacles that prevent people from engaging with life more intentionally. By using these techniques, you will be able to tap into your full potential and live a more joyful and fulfilling life. So, let's dive in and discover the power of engaging with reality more intentionally!

Technique One: Give Your Best Effort to Follow Form

When to Give Your Best Effort to Follow Form

Give your best effort to follow form in each moment in the areas of your life you care most about, have the strongest desire to fulfill, and where you want or need to be more successful. Although truthfully, there is no opportunity too small for this technique.

How to Give Your Best Effort to Follow Form

First, learn the best form to manifest and engage with an important part of your life in the way you truly want. To do this, identify someone who has demonstrated success in manifesting this aspect of their life the same way you want it. This person should be trustworthy, invested in your success, and know what they're talking about. If you don't have personal access to an expert who checks those boxes, find them in a book, a podcast, or online.

To "follow form" means to adhere to a blueprint that gives you the best chance of successfully manifesting a desired outcome. So, for example, for a runner, form is how you hold your body and use your breath. When you "follow form" during a run, you're ensuring that your whole self is in the best position to make your run successful. Just as a runner follows form to produce a successful run, you can do the same in any part of your life.

Once you identify someone you want to emulate, learn their form. Learn their success habits and best practices. Discover the foundation for their success and their pillars for manifesting this part of life so desirably. Find out how they live, how they spend their time, and their most helpful actions, ideas, attitudes, and focus.

Common examples of form include:

- How they care for themselves physically, emotionally, and mentally

- How they conduct themselves professionally and personally

- How they think and what they talk about

- How they get the most out of their time

- How they motivate themselves

- How they prepare themselves for success

- How they prioritize and organize their life

After you've learned the nuances of their form, adopt that form by giving your best effort to emulate it. Dedicate at least 150 minutes a week, or about 20 minutes a day, to specifically following their form in this part of your life. Practice their success habits and best practices, in each moment, even if no one would find out if you didn't.

You don't need to follow the form perfectly. All you need to do is give your best effort, in each moment, for at least two and a half hours a week. And anytime you notice you aren't giving 100 percent to following form, simply start doing so. Do not beat yourself up or try to make up for the moments you weren't following form; just gently remind yourself to follow form and start giving your best effort again.

If this part of your life is important enough to you, you can and should give your best effort to follow form. Why? Because this engagement technique is the surest way to take advantage of, and even expand, any opportunity to manifest and engage with reality as you desire.

If you struggle, remind yourself that your task isn't to do it perfectly. And who cares how many times you have to remind yourself to follow form? What matters is that you're giving your best effort at this moment.

Why Giving Your Best Effort to Follow Form Helps Your Performance

Going back to the running example, following form doesn't guarantee you'll run fast or far. In fact, sometimes following form can actually slow you down. Following form means you're inviting your whole self to the party. And giving your best effort positions you to produce the best possible versions of life. Giving your best effort to follow form helps your engagement with reality in at least four distinct ways:

- Following form assigns jobs to your whole self.

- Following form illuminates where help is needed.

- Following form gives you an internal litmus test.

- Following form takes pressure off.

Giving Your Best Effort to Follow Form Assigns Jobs to Your Whole Self

Giving your best effort to follow form invites your whole self to help your performance. Each part plays a vital role in your engagement with reality. Giving your best effort enlists each collaborator to support your performances.

As the CEO of your self, you have the most important job. A job where nothing can replace you fulfilling your responsibilities. Your ability to choose your actions, ideas, attitudes, and focus and follow through with them makes you the point person for identifying and following good form.

Your body has a role in helping you follow form as well. You may wind up asking it to help you by being better nourished, having greater resilience, getting more activity, keeping a persistent focus, and the like, so it can assist in making your engagement more successful.

Because you need help, especially from gatekeepers and authority figures, to engage successfully with reality, it's also appropriate to say that other people play a role in helping you follow form. It's always in your best interests to follow form regarding positively influencing others' opinions of you. Whenever it's possible to do so ethically, legally, and practically, meeting others' expectations is important.

It's true that some aspects of your life don't necessarily require this degree of attention because they're not important enough, but manifesting the big stuff almost always does. Giving your best effort to follow form helps get the right people "on the bus," so to speak, and then helps them find the "right seats." Any area of your life you care about is worthy of this level of attention.

Giving Your Best Effort to Follow Form Illuminates Where Help Is Needed

Even using this technique, you will still fall short of where you want to be. You will experience pain along the way. You'll encounter setbacks from challenges and difficulties, even when giving your best effort. And, since pain isn't the desired outcome, let's address that.

The two best ways to alleviate pain are to improve your form and put more effort into following it. And doing that requires knowing what, where, and how. By following form, you might learn that you need to get more sleep because your focus wanes every day around three o'clock. You may realize that you need to become more organized professionally because an important collaborator is dissatisfied with your output. Or you might discover that you need to work the belief-raising process you read about earlier because your life is unfulfilling.

Those examples illustrate how following form can help you identify the specific help you need. Your form provides a blueprint for how each part of your self should support giving your best effort. Knowing what your collaborators should be doing makes it easier to identify which of them needs to step up.

When every part of your self has been assigned their jobs, it is much easier to identify which parts need help and how. Because you know what each is supposed to be doing, you also know how they should be supporting your effort. When there's pain, you can usually tell which part was assigned to do that job.

Follow pain to its source, and you'll have some precise feedback and good solutions to try. You'll have a better chance of giving each component of your self the help it needs to join the party. You'll be able to issue very specific invitations to everyone and everything helping you.

Giving Your Best Effort to Follow Form Gives You an Internal Litmus Test

A vast array of factors negatively impacts the outcome of your efforts—the incapable beliefs you inherited, your family background, other people's prejudices, rules, expectations, and physical limitations, to name a few. You are not the sole determiner of how your material reality manifests; no matter how much effort you give, there will always be things affecting your life that are out of your control.

Thus, measuring your effectiveness by outcomes alone isn't fair. In fact, most of the time, it's a set-up for you to feel like a failure or beat yourself up. *"Am I satisfied with this part of my life, with the outcomes of my efforts?"* is an important question to ask yourself. But using the results of your efforts to answer it is too harsh because it forces you to take responsibility for things outside your control that are affecting those results.

A much kinder question is, *"Am I giving my best effort to follow form in this part of my life?"* When your answer to that question is no, all you need to do is start giving it. That's an easy and effective remedy. And there is no reason to berate yourself when your answer is no. There is no "lost ground" to make up. Simply remind yourself about your commitment and then give your best effort.

You're always in control of following your form, no matter the circumstances. And you're also in command of your effort, no matter what life throws at you. Best of all, this litmus test is always available. You're using something under your authority and gleaning answers you can use to adjust and regulate your engagement with reality. When you're not giving your best effort to follow form, the fix lies in your own hands.

Giving Your Best Effort to Follow Form Takes Pressure Off

Most of your life is public-facing, meaning others can tell what you're able (or unable) to accomplish. Therefore, you can be certain that other people will know when you're not successful. And when you're attempting to manifest the big stuff in your life, anticipating judgment can add pressure.

You can decide how you'll judge yourself, however. When you determine that giving your best effort to follow form constitutes success, you're using a kind, fair, and accurate litmus test. A litmus test that you can use privately and one that, when met, really does create the greatest chances of manifesting and engaging with reality as you desire.

Giving your best effort to follow form is the only thing you can do anyway. You can't dictate any other circumstances involved because you can only govern what *you* do. You should always do your best to positively influence other factors contributing to your life, but you don't get to prescribe them.

By not relying on the results of your efforts to gauge your effectiveness, you diminish the importance of others' judgments of you. If, for example, a neighbor still thinks poorly of you because the results of your efforts to take better care of your house have yet to materialize, that may be annoying, but their judgment no longer carries as much weight. Why not? Because you're no longer evaluating yourself on the criteria your neighbor is using—the public-facing results of your efforts.

There is no reason to focus on manifesting your life a certain way versus simply giving your best effort to follow form. Usually, the less pressure you feel, the better your results anyway. Freed from actual and imagined scrutiny, you discover a sense of truly having nothing to lose. Without the stress of having only two possible outcomes, success or failure, you will actually find it easier to hit the target.

Technique Two: Satisfy Your Critic

When to Satisfy Your Critic

Satisfy your critic when you're being directly criticized about an important part of your life—especially when the critics' opinions matter to you or when satisfying their expectations is necessary. This technique involves satisfying your critic regardless of whether you agree with the criticism, but it's especially valuable when you don't.

How to Satisfy Your Critic

First, make sure you have a crystal clear understanding of the criticism. Without refuting it or defending yourself, find out from your critic's perspective exactly where and how you're falling short. Then learn precisely how to satisfy your critic's expectations of you and your performance in this area.

Sometimes you are your own critic. Self-criticism is usually the harshest, least understanding criticism you receive. You can use this technique with internal criticism the exact same way as with the external variety. It works just as well with both categories to help you deliver your best performances.

Next, as long as your critic's expectations are reasonable, appropriate, legal, moral, and ethical, let your critic know how you will address the issue. Be open with your critic and also with a trustworthy third party and share what expectations you're satisfying and how you will do so. This way, you, your critic, and the third party can all see and verify when those expectations have been met.

Then, finally, follow through and satisfy your critic's expectations of you in this part of your life. Again, strive to meet their expectations as long as they are reasonable, appropriate, legal, moral, and ethical. Improve your form and invest more effort until you've done so.

Why Satisfying Your Critic Helps Your Performance

Satisfying your critic tremendously helps your performances in at least four unique ways. This technique won't guarantee you'll manifest and engage with your reality exactly as you desire, but it guarantees you'll have good directions. It also allows you to sidestep any self-delusion about the adequacy of your form and effort by enlisting some motivated watchdogs.

Satisfying your critic:

- Productively employs almost anyone

- Reveals blind spots

- Works with any critic

- Separates haters from allies

Satisfying Your Critic Separates Haters from Allies

When you meet your critic's reasonable expectations, your critic should be satisfied. And since you've also shared what you're doing with a third party, there can be no denying when you've successfully done so. In fact, your critic might even respond by becoming an ally because it's inspiring to watch someone overcome obstacles and succeed.

Everyone involved knew how you were going to satisfy your critic's expectations. You were transparent about what you would do, and everyone agreed ahead of time on how your accomplishments would be verified. And now that you've met them, at a minimum, the problem is resolved and your critic is appeased.

If this is not how your critic responds, however, it means their criticism was fraudulent and merely a cover for some hidden agenda. While that surely isn't a pleasant outcome, you will have at least outed a hater. You'll have revealed this person to be dishonest and someone you can probably ignore from now on. Haters are fakes who refuse to be satisfied because their criticism of you goes much deeper than you need to care about. They are people whose criticism is directed at you for reasons you can't do anything about. You always want to know who falls into this category so you can ignore them.

In this manner, satisfying your critic lets you know who your true allies are. You learn who was being a constructive critic, which means they are at least somewhat trustworthy, invested in you, and knowledgeable. Constructive critics can be invaluable team members; identify them so you can be even more intentional about enlisting their help moving forward.

Satisfying Your Critic Productively Employs Almost Anyone

Criticism is usually not fun to hear, but it happens. If you're not receiving it occasionally, you're probably playing it too safe. Hopefully, the criticism you receive is constructive and comes from people who know what they're talking about, but even criticism delivered by haters can contain some truth you need to hear.

Constructive criticism meets two important criteria:

1. It is being levied at you to help you.

2. It usually turns out to be something you would benefit from addressing.

A hater fails the first criterion. But a hater's criticism can still meet the second.

When your critic's expectations are reasonable, meeting them will almost always be good for you and your life. You'll never regret resolving criticism. Even if the critic is revealed to be a hater afterward, you can still benefit from the positive, helpful changes you made.

Whichever category your critic falls into, ally or hater, satisfying their criticism benefits you either way. It makes you more productive and effective in that area of your life. And it demonstrates public-facing success along the way too, increasing the odds of them manifesting a more favorable image of you in their reality. This makes it all the more likely that other people, some of whom you might not have even known were paying attention, may want to help you and invest in your success.

In this manner, satisfying your critic employs anyone who cares enough to criticize you. You don't need to predetermine which category they fall into because they'll categorize themselves after you meet their expectations. By focusing on meeting their expectations rather than discerning their motives, you're an equal-opportunity employer.

Satisfying Your Critic Reveals Blind Spots

Blind spots are the worst. They make your life difficult and painful, yet you don't even know they're there. And it's next to impossible to resolve a problem you don't even know you have.

Learning about your blind spots is rarely enjoyable, but it's vital for your success. There is almost no way you can be aware of everything about yourself. Even the most self-actualized humans have blind spots and cognitive dissonance—the distance between how they see themselves and how the rest of the world sees them.

This technique is important because humans tend to protect and maintain their blind spots. This quirk is illustrated perfectly by the fact the term "disillusion" carries a negative connotation for most. As a person for whom achieving a more pleasing version of reality is important, you don't want to rely solely on yourself to identify problem areas.

Satisfying your critic allows you to address any problems that will be in your best interests to solve. Perhaps it's a problem you're aware of but simply haven't been willing to tackle. This technique helps you with issues you might not know about or are unaware of how important resolving them might be.

When intentionally manifesting and engaging with your reality, transparency and accountability work magic. Satisfying your critic checks both of those boxes. By addressing something about yourself that's a problem in someone else's eyes, whether you agree or not, you voluntarily expose yourself to an added layer of transparency and accountability.

Satisfying Your Critic Works with Any Critic

Hopefully, you have the occasional critic who cares enough to expect the best from you. Because not everyone has that privilege, celebrate those people!

The majority of your critics will likely be constructive ones who are doing their best to help you succeed. But rest assured, satisfying your critic works whether they're trying to help you or are hiding a different agenda. The ability to separate the two is a big part of this technique's value.

Thankfully, this technique works just as well with self-criticism because it's vital to resolve self-criticism for the same reasons you should satisfy other critics. Often, however, the most challenging critic to categorize will be you. It's helpful to distinguish constructive self-criticism from self-hating, both of which appear as worry, self-doubt, regret, and fear.

Resolving self-criticism frees you from the confusion and ineffectiveness created by inadvertently treating your inner hater like a constructive critic. Any painful feelings nudging you to give better effort or to improve your form are self-criticisms of the constructive variety. Torturing yourself with painful feelings without changing those things, however, is being a self-hater. You can effectively ignore haters—even when it's you!

What to Do If Criticism Is Indirect

When you receive criticism secondhand, you can still use this technique. When that happens, I highly recommend you simply tell the messenger:

"Thanks for your concern, but will you do me a favor? From now on, anytime you hear anything like that about me, please tell them that I'd like to hear from them directly. Please tell them I want to learn exactly what they're seeing, straight from the horse's mouth, so I can address it."

And from that point on, you can effectively ignore any secondhand criticism supposedly coming from that critic.

It's vital for criticism to be delivered firsthand, and appropriate to ignore it when it's not, for at least two reasons:

- The messenger's filters change the criticism.

- You don't need to care about a supposed problem more than a critic does.

The Messenger's Filters Change the Message

Even if a messenger does their best to relay, verbatim, someone else's criticisms, they cannot escape their own filters. Their relationship with you and what they believe about you will dictate what they share and how they share it. The messenger's agenda regarding what's most important, what you most need to know, and how it should be framed will almost always differ from the critic's.

The messenger is not necessarily wrong nor ill-intended in their determinations, but they simply cannot be as accurate with the information as the critic. And when satisfying your critic, accuracy is a top priority. All parties must be on the same page regarding what the problems are and how they will be addressed to everyone's satisfaction.

You Don't Need to Care about a Problem More than Your Critic

If a critic doesn't want to tell you about the problem directly, it means one of two things. Either the critic doesn't actually care that much or they're pre-identifying themselves as a hater. Either way, it's healthier not to respond to secondhand criticism.

You're not dodging the issue here either. If everything is aboveboard, the critic's messenger will relay your desire to personally speak with them. If the issue is important enough, the critic will come see you or communicate with you directly in another way. In the meantime, you have much more important uses for your time and energy.

Technique Three: Use Your Board of Directors

When to Use Your Board of Directors

Use your board of directors whenever you are trying to manifest and engage with the most important parts of your life as you truly desire, especially with essential public-facing manifestations where others can readily see whether or not you're successful. This technique will help you gather the most trustworthy, invested, and qualified helpers.

How to Use Your Board of Directors

First, identify a small group of people you have access to who have the highest levels of trustworthiness, investment in you, and expertise in the area you're focusing on. These folks should be willing to help you succeed and readily equipped with relevant experience, connections, and resources. Keep it around three or four people because you'll be meeting with each of them once a month.

These should be people with whom you have personal access. You want face-to-face meetings with them, or at least phone access, because they will be advising and helping you with some of the most significant parts of your life. And all your board members should earn their seats through their qualifications. Your reliance on them for key advice and help means you should never seat someone on your board just because of their relationship with or proximity to you.

Next, formally ask each person you identified if they are willing to get personally involved in your success. Ask them if they are willing to meet with you regularly to discuss your form, review your efforts to follow it, and evaluate the results you're getting. Ask them to hold you accountable for following through too. Be up front with them, sharing what you're doing, how you're doing it, and how they can help you. If someone declines your invitation, simply take it as a sign that it's probably not a good match right now and move on to your next candidate.

Then, once you have gotten buy-in from invitees, start using your board of directors by meeting with each of them on a regular basis. The meeting will usually be dictated by everyone's availability, but aim to meet with each board member at least once a month. Between meetings, share any relevant, pertinent information with your board members to keep them in the loop. The more they know before your in-person meetings, the more direct, personalized, and helpful their involvement and feedback can be.

Your entire purpose for being together is to learn and grow under the invested mentoring of someone trustworthy who knows what they're talking about. Your goal in every exchange with a board member is to be as transparent as possible about the form you're following, the effort you're giving, and the results of those efforts. Additionally, make yourself accountable to your board members for authentically delivering on those things. Do not defend your actions, ideas, attitudes, and focus in response to their critiques and questions; only explain to clarify. When communicating with a board member, listen twice as much as you speak.

The final step for using this technique is to use your board members' feedback to adjust your form and your effort as needed. Put their guidance into action by following through on it. Knowing you'll be meeting again soon will give you extra motivation to do this.

It's very common to have one board member who is more trustworthy, invested in your success, and equipped to help you than any other. It's natural for this person to become your primary mentor or coach, someone you turn to most readily for assistance. Don't neglect the value your other board members provide, but feel free to lean in to one whose investment in you rises above the others.

Why Using Your Board of Directors Helps Your Performance

Using your board of directors is a phenomenal way to improve your performance in at least four effective ways. This technique won't guarantee you'll always achieve the life you desire, but you'll always have high-quality guidance. Additionally, you'll be assured of positive pressure to follow through on your goals.

Using your board of directors:

- Gets the right people in the right seats on the bus

- Directs your attention to those whose opinions matter most

- Utilizes the power of two

- Allows your advisers to grow with you

Using Your Board of Directors Gets the Right People in the Right Seats on the Bus

Having a board of directors is your ongoing opportunity to curate the most important people in your life. Who are the most trustworthy people you have access to? Who is truly invested in your success and knows what the heck they're talking about? Who are the people who've been there and done that?

These are authority figures and gatekeepers to whom you have personal access—the most accomplished and successful folks, those with power and influence, who are willing to invest in your success. You're tasked with being discerning enough not to invite anyone to your board without those qualifications. Being a friend, family member, or neighbor doesn't, in and of itself, make someone a good candidate.

Trustworthy, invested, high-quality people are exactly who you need on your bus to manifest the big stuff. And putting your most powerful collaborators in the right seats allows you to take the best advantage of their strengths, maximizes everyone's time, and helps them help you.

Leverage your transparency and accountability while interacting with your board of directors. Position them to help you shape your goals and your plans to manifest those goals. Embrace their expertise. At regular intervals, use their feedback about your results to improve every aspect of your manifesting and engagement.

Using Your Board of Directors Directs Your Attention to Those Whose Opinions Matter Most

Caring too much about what other people think affects almost every human at some point. It's notorious for causing stress—especially when their opinions and criticisms are not constructive or their evaluation of you is unfair. Caring about what others think can create anxiety and cause unnecessary self-doubt.

Ironically, one of the best ways to stop caring about what people think about you is actually to care about it *more*. If you want to care less about some people's opinions of you, become more intentional about whose opinions you *do* care about. And then double down on meeting the expectations of *those* people.

Using your board of directors does this for you. You've got the right people on your bus now—people important enough to your success that you should care about what they think of you. Your board members are trustworthy, invested, and knowledgeable enough for this status, so satisfying them should be a high priority for you.

Using Your Board of Directors Utilizes the Power of Two

Using your board of directors provides further emphasis on how integral other people are to your manifesting and engagement. A special energy arises when connecting with someone you're willing to listen to and learn from—the energy of me, the Quantum Field. Being transparent with and accountable to another person about something important gives rise to my presence in a way that cannot be replicated by other means.

Being transparent with and accountable to someone else about significant things can be messy. It often upsets the status quo, it's usually challenging, and it will definitely take you out of your comfort zone. In fact, most humans will choose not to do it for those reasons. Not engaging with someone else allows you to avoid some of those frustrations but at the cost of not manifesting my greater presence through your connection with them.

Sharing with another person, to learn from them and grow, creates a special kind of magic. It's similar to a phenomenon in music, where two notes played in harmony give birth to a third note that doesn't exist outside of that harmony. When you are transparent with and accountable to another person, the two of you birth a third energy that doesn't exist outside of that connection—me. I am able to join in directly!

The deeper you dive into transparency and accountability, the more clearly I can make my presence felt. I will help both of you find helpful perspectives to consider and share. I'll encourage you to listen more than talk and remind you to ask questions to learn rather than to defend yourself. I'll ensure you have the best potential to assimilate and actualize the feedback you get.

Using Your Board of Directors Allows Your Advisors to Grow with You

As your life comes into greater alignment with your desires, you will naturally notice an ongoing need for new guidance. You're now manifesting parts of your life in ways some of your current board members are no longer qualified to help you with. Even when they're still trustworthy and invested in you, you may have outpaced their expertise.

Success, which your efforts will invariably produce in some measure, opens you up to new advisors. Public-facing success attracts the attention and interest of people who are correspondingly more trustworthy, invested, and knowledgeable. Success leads people to manifest versions of you that are more compelling to help and invest in. The change in your advisors is both a validation of your efforts and a boon to it.

Let your success guide your board membership. You will understand that more is possible each time you manifest a more aligned version of reality. With the growth of your desires comes the need for even more qualified board members. Just as you give yourself permission to dream bigger, you should also give yourself permission to be advised by even more qualified people.

Greater success attracts people more capable of helping you, and greater desires need those types of folks. As you come into contact with people more qualified to advise you, do not be afraid to expand your board or replace board members. Your board of directors is for you alone; you *should* be selfish (but not self-centered) about who sits on it. Conveying your love, friendship, and respect for someone does not require seating them on your board.

Technique Four: Create a Positive Checkmate

When to Create a Positive Checkmate

Create a positive checkmate when manifesting and engaging with something so important that you want to proactively eliminate your ability to quietly quit later. Use this technique when success is expected of you, by you, and by others, so you have no other option but to keep giving your best effort.

How to Create a Positive Checkmate

Let me explain the use of the term "checkmate" here. Checkmate occurs in the game of chess when a player's king cannot move. Checkmate means someone has their opponent's king trapped. Here though, it's not an opponent's king you're checkmating, it's you! When the going gets rough and you're tempted to give up on something very important, you want to be in checkmate.

To checkmate yourself, first identify the people most adamant that you need to be more successful in this area of your life—people with a vested interest in your success and who are most likely to notice such changes. Ideally, these people are also trustworthy and knowledgeable.

Next, be transparent with these people about what part of your life you're going to manifest differently, how, and why. Talk to them about the purpose of these changes and what you expect to accomplish. Tell them how you'll be doing it differently so they can verify your public-facing successes and you can create accountability for yourself by committing to doing it.

Then, hold yourself accountable for manifesting and engaging with your reality differently, just as you told them you would. Give your best effort to follow good form, satisfy your critics, and use your board of directors—use all the techniques wherever they fit. And let the resulting accountability you created be an additional source of motivation and inspiration.

Why Creating a Positive Checkmate Helps Your Performance

Creating a positive checkmate is a remarkable way to help ensure your best performance in at least four unique ways. When applied in such a positive way, the weight of accountability can move mountains over time, let alone help you get out of bed each morning. This technique does not guarantee you'll manifest and engage with reality exactly as desired, but it does ensure that you won't give up easily.

Creating a positive checkmate:

- Burns the bridges

- Ensures your best possible effort

- Utilizes the power of two

- Deepens relationships

Creating a Positive Checkmate Burns the Bridges

When success is the only acceptable option in a specific part of your life, you're naturally more willing to give your very best effort. But despite those best efforts, you know that the path to success is rarely a straight line. You will certainly encounter many unexpected roadblocks and challenges along the way.

When the difficulties on the path become scary, when they challenge your confidence, your resolve will be tested too. Depending on the size and scope of the obstacles, it can be tempting to walk away rather than try to "slay the dragon." You may even try to convince yourself that the desire isn't really that important anymore.

While there is nothing wrong with reassessing your desires and your path, when it comes to the most essential parts of your life, it's almost always more appropriate to continue forward. There is no reliable mechanism for stopping the desire to succeed in the most significant areas of your life—your health, wealth, fitness, love, relationships, career, etc. Those parts of life are simply too integral to human fulfillment.

A positive checkmate occurs when you create public accountability—when you tell important allies and involved partners what you're going to do, why you're going to do it, and how you will do it. A positive checkmate, quite simply, does nothing short of making yourself accountable to the people you want or need to satisfy. Bailing out if you encounter obstacles will become more difficult after such disclosure.

Creating a positive checkmate restricts your ability to disengage. It burns the bridges you might've used to quietly retreat, returning to whence you came. And when your life is that important to you, you'll be grateful that option isn't as easy to employ when the path gets rocky.

Creating a Positive Checkmate Ensures Your Best Possible Effort

This technique is for parts of your life essential enough to your fulfillment that you don't want to be chased away by problems and challenges. You don't want to be able to depart easily if the path suddenly gets a lot harder. A positive checkmate allows you to intentionally craft a level of accountability that removes your ripcord. You can still step away, but you'll now need to do so publicly.

Because of the public accountability you intentionally created, you're not going anywhere. So you might as well continue intentionally manifesting and engaging with your reality. Given the challenges on your path, actualizing it certainly requires that intention.

Courage is not only the absence of fear; it's also the resolve to move forward despite it. Creating a positive checkmate gives you courage in the face of difficult challenges. Because you've removed the option of succumbing, you have almost no choice but to give your best effort in spite of whatever challenges arise.

Creating a Positive Checkmate Utilizes the Power of Two

Other people wield tremendous influence over your life. Much of changing your life involves taking positive advantage of their significance by making yourself transparent and accountable to them. And this technique is fashioned to help you do all that.

Creating a positive checkmate also involves others by invoking my greater presence because it's about connecting. When you are transparent with and accountable to another person, your connection gives birth to my presence in a way that cannot be duplicated. You have invoked me.

My presence helps you listen to learn. I'll help you put down the stick and stop beating yourself up when the feedback you get isn't what you wanted. I'll assist you in staying focused on using the feedback from your feelings to improve your form and give greater effort to follow it. The greater your transparency and the deeper your accountability, the stronger my presence will be.

I enjoy immediate personal communication with you, so creating a positive checkmate is one of my favorite techniques. It virtually guarantees I can have a strong, impactful presence. Your connection with the other person not only invokes the power of this technique, it also invokes my greater presence while doing so.

Creating a Positive Checkmate Deepens Relationships

Not everyone you make yourself accountable to will be a preexisting ally. But they are all interested, involved parties—people who are likely to benefit from your success. You have a relationship with all these folks, and often, some of them wield authority that can impact your life.

The act of creating a positive checkmate is an impressive and essential step. It shows people that you understand the importance of success in this part of your life. And because the folks you're creating accountability with are interested and involved, they will undoubtedly agree with the emphasis you're giving it.

The mere act of creating a positive checkmate deepens others' respect for you. And following through by giving your best effort inspires their trust. At a minimum, those things display your self-awareness, capacity, and agency and will increase others' regard and esteem for you.

Since providing accountability isn't required of you, this technique helps people realize better versions of you in their realities. Those already invested in you will strengthen those ties. And even if you don't create new allies, you will almost always cause people to reconsider the meaning and value you hold in their realities. All of these are potential motivations for them to offer you help and invest in your success.

Technique Five: Manifest a Penny

When to Manifest a Penny

Manifest a penny when you want to have more money (or anything else, actually), especially when it's an important public-facing part of your life. Use this technique before you have the confidence born of successfully manifesting money or anything else you truly want.

How to Manifest a Penny

First, intentionally manifest a penny. It's child's play, after all. You can find a penny virtually anywhere—on the ground, sidewalk, parking lot, path, or floor and not be surprised by it because nobody cares about them. Pennies are so worthless people simply throw them away.

Don't strain to find a penny; just let one be there. Don't "hawkeye" the penny, "needing" to manifest one. Instead, enjoy finding it. Practice knowing a penny is there and simply discovering it. There's really no pressure because manifesting one isn't actually going to fulfill your money desires anyway.

Next, pick up the penny and hold it in your hand. Squeeze the penny, feeling its weight and substance—it's real. Engage with it based on what it symbolizes—a reminder of how effortlessly I, the Quantum Field, co-create with you. Celebrate how easily I can create something as simple as money. It is more than a literal and tangible emblem of the money you desire; it represents the energies of abundance, possibility, potential, opportunity, infinite creativity, and ease.

Privately sing the praises of this penny. Celebrate, in grand fashion, the energy of what that penny represents: financial abundance. Say *Thank you!* and sing songs glorifying this token of financial abundance. Don't hold back; covertly go over the top! You're not exalting the *amount* of money you've just produced; you're gushing over how this penny reminds you of my infinite abundance, unbridled creativity, the ease and effortless simplicity of my creations, and my unlimited ability to create anything with you, especially money.

Here is an example of Greg Kuhn celebrating a penny he manifested. Notice how his exaltations had nothing to do with the amount of money:

Thank you for reminding me that abundance is child's play! Thank you for reminding me that scarcity is a lie, a lie that exists only in my mind! Abundance is my birthright! Thank you for reminding me that anything is possible and that the only thing separating me from money are incapable beliefs and inadequate engagement. At any time, you and I can manifest anything! Thank you for reminding me of all that!

You're buzzing! Carry that raised energy with you for as long as you can. You are now genuinely aligned with and grateful for money, even though you haven't yet acquired the amount you truly desire.

Your celebrations are authentic because the penny really does represent all that you're attributing to it. And your energy will be aligned not only with money for a while afterward but with the energy of abundance, creativity, possibility, ease, and success as well. Unleash your connection with my infinite creativity for the rest of your day, and continue using that energy to manifest money (and abundance in all forms) for as long as you can.

You can use this technique on virtually any desire. Simply find a suitable token of your desire that is easy to actualize. Select a symbol that, like a penny, is not seen as inherently valuable but can be celebrated as a genuine representation of what you desire. It might be seeing beautiful sunrises when hoping for better health, finding heart shapes when wanting more love, or spotting joggers when aiming for greater fitness. Then, when you manifest that token, engage with it based on what it represents, just as you would do after manifesting a penny.

Why Manifesting a Penny Helps Your Performance

Manifesting a penny is a tremendous help to your performances in at least four special ways. The best way to manifest something, of course, is to already <u>be</u> manifesting it. The confidence and skill that come along with this make it relatively easy to *keep* manifesting. Manifesting a penny gives you that same kind of energy before you're really creating it by manifesting the money you truly desire. It isn't a guarantee you'll call forth the exact amount of money you really want, but it aligns you with the gratitude-energy of authentic financial abundance.

Manifesting a penny:

- Is an easy and repeatable win

- Creates authentic celebrations and gratitude

- Helps you manifest more money

- Is an evergreen practice

Manifesting a Penny Is an Easy and Repeatable Win

Could any amount of money be easier to attract than a penny? In fact, pennies might be the easiest single thing to manifest. There are pennies everywhere. Even when you're not intentionally looking for them, you see them all the time.

A penny isn't going to fulfill your desire for money, so there's no pressure on you to find one. When you look down and there isn't a penny, who cares? You need a lot more than one penny to manifest the amount of money you desire, so it's okay that you aren't manifesting one right now. Remind yourself that there's no deadline to meet. Let it go and get back to practicing knowing that you can and will manifest a penny.

Attracting something this attainable, with energetic value far surpassing its monetary worth, is a perfect embodiment of low-hanging fruit. You get to experience the immediate and authentic success that is directly connected to bringing about more of what you desire. Even if you aren't manifesting a penny right now, you will soon enough, and nothing breeds success like success.

You also build your overall manifesting efficacy when you manifest a penny. Every time you do, your confidence in your ability to affect reality as you desire is strengthened. And simultaneously, you get to rev up your connection with the energy of financial abundance. Manifesting a penny is like having ready access to free shots of "prosperity espresso."

Manifesting a Penny Creates Authentic Celebrations and Gratitude

There is no manifesting fuel as powerful as authentic gratitude. Genuine celebration usually ensures you'll attract something because being authentically grateful for it typically only occurs when you're already in possession of it. Nothing helps you manifest a desired version of reality more than already manifesting it that way.

This technique is similar to reverse engineering, which is normally virtually impossible to experience before you're manifesting reality the way you want. But if you have authentic gratitude and genuine celebration before you manifest something as truly desired, you get to manifest it, right now, as if you've already been doing it. This is invaluable help, especially in parts of your life where you've been disappointed.

You engage with the penny based on what it represents, not on how much it's worth. And what it represents is truly worth celebrating when you allow it to remind you of my unlimited and infinite creativity, abundance, power, collaboration, potential, knowledge, and possibilities. You can always genuinely celebrate a penny for representing those things. It's a rational display of gratitude applied appropriately to your penny.

Manifesting a Penny Helps You Manifest More Money

Although this technique focuses on pennies, the energy infusion around money leads to creating larger amounts. Your actions, ideas, attitudes, and focus toward attracting money will grow more inspired, which almost always leads to manifesting much more money than one cent.

Holding a coin that you've just intentionally manifested is quite empowering. It is a lived experience that your subconscious won't ignore because of its authenticity. Which means your subconscious embraces your private celebrations of that penny and influences your beliefs about money.

Obviously, attracting the amount of money you truly desire requires you to manifest more than just a penny. But you're not using this technique to become rich one penny at a time. You're using it so that you engage with money in more inspired and aligned ways. Your engagement allows pennies to help you select helpful actions, ideas, attitudes, and focus surrounding money that have a higher potential for success.

Keep manifesting pennies, and you'll become more capable of manifesting money. Allow what you learn to grow the capacity of your decisions. The sharper your insight into what it takes to bring about larger amounts of money, the higher the probability of success.

Manifesting a Penny Is an Evergreen Practice

Manifesting a penny is evergreen because you can do it anywhere, any place, and any time. There's always the possibility of a penny lying around, so it's always believable that you can find one. Whether you're focused on seeing one in the moment or not, finding a penny will rarely surprise you.

Manifesting a penny is also evergreen because it is a great way to practice manifesting specific things. It's possible to manifest virtually anything else, intentionally and on command. Manifesting a penny is so enjoyable and rewarding to practice, it might not be long before you're applying this skill in other ways.

Materializing something specific, like a penny, is a skill you improve with practice. Like lifting weights, your manifesting muscles get stronger with quality repetitions. The better you get at manifesting a penny, the stronger your manifesting muscles will grow. And with successful practice, your beliefs will expand the scope and size of places you'll most likely find pennies.

Manifesting on command like this requires a strong and unique connection with me, the Quantum Field. As long as it's foundationally believable to manifest something, you can do it. The skills you hone while manifesting pennies apply to manifesting virtually anything else similarly attainable.

Our manifesting connection is so personal that I cannot state, specifically, how each human will do it. But I can share that manifesting an object on command, whether a penny, sunrise, heart shapes, or joggers, involves walking the line between needing to see it and allowing yourself to see it. Manifesting on demand involves navigating the difference between demanding its presence and allowing its presence to delight you.

Technique Six: Use a Positive Affirmation

When to Use a Positive Affirmation

Use a positive affirmation under two circumstances: When you've gotten off track in an area of life where you're usually successful, or when you're nervous about delivering a performance you're well prepared for—especially when you've experienced success in this area before or have reasonable expectations for success now. Use this technique to get yourself out of a provisional rut or to resolve a temporary lack of confidence.

How to Use a Positive Affirmation

When you find yourself off track or feeling less confident, using a positive affirmation is all about telling the best-feeling, most believable story about you, your abilities, and the situation. A positive affirmation is a private pep talk designed to get you back on track and restore your confidence. In such instances, a positive affirmation is a bracing and welcomed reminder.

Examples of positive affirmations include:

"I am a strong, capable leader who listens to the people I supervise." (Use something like this when you're feeling worried about leading a potentially contentious meeting at work.)

"I am a beautiful person, inside and out." (Say something like this when you're feeling ugly after getting teased.)

"I am ready for this. I'm well-prepared, and I know what I'm doing. I'm gonna kill it out there!" (The perfect pep talk when you're feeling nervous about giving a TED Talk.)

Using a positive affirmation is an intentional reallocation of your attitudes and focus onto positive expectations that you already authentically possess. Quietly and privately remind yourself about your true, capable beliefs and your very real capacity for successful engagement.

Even when they don't chase away challenging circumstances, positive affirmations reconnect you with pertinent attributes, your track record, and previous successful experiences.

These uplifting pep talks should be based on your <u>actual</u> beliefs and experiences. Your stories should not only feel good, but they should also be <u>believable</u>. You're not inventing these better-feeling perspectives; you're reminding yourself of ones already present and possible. If this is not the case, you're probably facing a situation best addressed using another technique.

Why Using a Positive Affirmation Helps Your Performance

Using a positive affirmation helps you give your best performance in at least four beneficial ways. You never know when things will get rough in life, but you know they will. You'll face challenges regularly that throw you off your game. Using a positive affirmation is a handy and readily available reminder of the alignment between your beliefs and your desires. While this technique cannot guarantee you will successfully manifest reality as you desire, it is often a great way to engage reality.

Using a positive affirmation:

- Gets you back on track

- Inspires action

- Feels good

- Helps identify incapable inherited beliefs

Using a Positive Affirmation Gets You Back on Track

Being off track means you were on the track previously. When you simply need a reminder that you're usually on track but have slipped off it for whatever reason, a positive affirmation can do the trick. It's a strong reminder that you're capable and equipped to actualize reality as you desire in this part of your life.

Life is guaranteed to throw you curveballs. Because so much of your material reality and your experience of it is influenced and affected by factors outside your control, you know you'll regularly encounter challenging conditions. Loss and failure will occur along the way, often knocking you off track. Remembering that you actually *belong* back on that track is an important part of getting back on it.

It's natural for painful versions of reality to make you question things, especially when it appears you are to blame for them because of a mistake, misstep, or failure. Every human slips, and you all have moments when you could have done better. The pain of self-abuse in situations like this can be mitigated, however, by reminding yourself when these results are not indicative of your normal capacity.

A positive affirmation is an appropriate pep talk from your more reasonable inner coach—the one detached from the pain you're suffering. The words come from your reservoir of lived experience, your inner knowing that your true beliefs are much more capable than the life you're experiencing at the moment. While it might not instantly put you back on track, a positive affirmation gets you pointed in the right direction.

Using a Positive Affirmation Inspires Action

You are the decider, in charge of your actions. Your beliefs set the stage, but you are the one in control of how you engage with reality upon it. And when your life becomes painful, especially when it is unnecessarily so, it often becomes more challenging to manage control over your engagement. Undesirable versions of reality can snatch the steering wheel right out of your hands.

Ideas, attitudes, and focus inspire actions. But coming up with potent actions under less-than-ideal circumstances can be like swimming against the current. While they don't dictate what you do, lower-quality ideas, attitudes, and focus make it more challenging to devise effective actions and follow through on them.

When actions are inspired by more aligned ideas, attitudes, and focus, however, you start to swim downstream. Under those circumstances, actions appear as the next right thing to do. You more readily understand their connection to changing how you're manifesting and engaging with reality. You're no longer trying to hammer a square peg into a round hole simply because it's "supposed" to go there.

When you use a positive affirmation to remind yourself of the success you usually enjoy in an area of your life, you are exerting your hegemony over your ideas, attitudes, and focus. You are redirecting yourself to your authentically aligned beliefs in this part of your life, as demonstrated by previous success there. A positive affirmation is like a pause button, allowing you to remember the reasons you normally expect more from a situation like this.

Using a Positive Affirmation Feels Good

A positive internal dialogue usually feels good. And it certainly feels better than whatever circumstances and feelings prompted you to deliberately deliver it in the first place. Even when a positive affirmation is not actually growing incompatible inherited beliefs into alignment, what's wrong with feeling good?

Pay attention to whether or not the positive affirmation adequately improves the painful situation. If it doesn't, simply note that you're most likely dealing with incapable beliefs and/or inadequate engagement—things best addressed in ways other than positive affirmations. That doesn't mean, however, that you can't give yourself a positive pep talk in the meantime.

Don't use a positive affirmation unless you're feeling bad about things. You don't need to remind yourself that you are worthy, capable, lovable, and valuable when you already feel that way. You don't intentionally craft positive affirmations when things are going well, right? So use a positive affirmation whenever you want to feel better.

The ability to reframe your internal dialogue in more constructive and supportive terms is tremendously valuable. Even when not technically growing incapable beliefs into alignment with your desires, it still allows you to feel good in the moment. And while it may not be possible to feel good every moment, you'll never regret allowing yourself to feel as good as you can.

Using a Positive Affirmation Helps Identify Incapable Inherited Beliefs

If you spill a glass of water, a towel will easily clean up the mess. But if the water is coming from a leaking pipe under your sink, you'll need more than a towel to fix the problem. You have to actually repair the pipe to remedy a leak.

Think of a positive affirmation as a towel. Spilled water represents getting off track or feeling needlessly unsure of yourself. And a leaky pipe symbolizes having incapable beliefs and/or inadequate engagement. Towels are the perfect clean-up tool for the right situations, but the key is employing them properly. Use positive affirmations on spills, not leaks, and you're playing to their strengths.

Because of this difference, positive affirmations can actually alert you to the presence of incapable beliefs and inadequate engagement. They can serve as a red-light warning signal, calling your attention to some beliefs you might want to realign and adjust. When you encounter the pain of being off track, it means you know your life shouldn't be as painful as it is. So you get yourself back on track by using a positive affirmation.

If you find that you're almost always off that track, you're probably dealing with a leak instead of a spill. When positive affirmations are the main thing keeping this part of your life afloat or aren't really working, you have undoubtedly pulled the veil back on some incongruent beliefs and/or inadequate engagement. And now you know what to do next.

Technique Seven: Make a Manifesting Mount Rushmore

When to Make a Manifesting Mount Rushmore

Make a manifesting Mount Rushmore in the most important parts of your life, such as health, love, wealth, fitness, and relationships, especially when you've struggled to manifest that part of your life as you really want. Use this technique to unleash the immense positive power of collaboration and interdependence upon any version of reality you want or need to manifest differently.

How to Make a Manifesting Mount Rushmore

First, decide what you want to manifest using broad terminology. To the best of your ability, articulate your desire as a state of being rather than a specific accomplishment. For example, specify a desire for "wealth" rather than "one million dollars." Or "love" rather than a "soulmate." Or "fitness" rather than a "beach body."

Next, decide upon four ways to best elicit and experience that desire. Do this by identifying four accomplishments that will collectively evoke the state of being you selected.

These four accomplishments will be the giant, sculpted US presidents' heads on your manifesting Mount Rushmore.

So first, choose your desired state of being and then pick the top four ways you wish to evoke it. For example, if you desire wealth, you might select the following four accomplishments to be on your manifesting Mount Rushmore:

- Money

- Valuable skills

- Knowledge and experience

- Collaboration with successful people

Or "a soulmate, intimacy, trust, and accountability" could be the four ways you elicit your desire for love. And your health goals might be fulfilled through "fitness, being active, healthy biometric data, and less physical pain."

Then, give your best effort to intentionally manifest each of those four accomplishments. Apply any and all of the previously described techniques early and often in your quest to achieve your goals. Learn the form used by people who are successfully manifesting each one as you desire and give your best effort to follow it in each of those parts of your life for at least 150 minutes a week (and more if possible).

The key to this technique is that each of the four accomplishments comprising your manifesting Mount Rushmore be of equal importance. Holding yourself accountable for all four equally spreads the wealth, responsibility, and pressure. None of the four ever plays second fiddle to the other three, and each receives your best efforts at all times. You'll find that when one experience excels, it symbiotically helps grow the other three. The four accomplishments are interdependent, meaning they complement and flesh out the others.

Why Making a Manifesting Mount Rushmore Helps Your Performance

Making a manifesting Mount Rushmore powerfully enhances your engagement with reality in at least four ways. The shared responsibility not only eases pressure on any one part of your path to success, but it also makes actualizing your desire much more likely and possible. While you will cherish manifesting any of the four experiences alone, together they form success beyond the mere sum total of their parts.

Making a manifesting Mount Rushmore:

- Spreads the wealth

- Distributes the responsibilities

- Lowers the pressure

- Mirrors how you manifest reality

Making a Manifesting Mount Rushmore Spreads the Wealth

Nature gives you a great example of this technique's power: a rising tide. When the tide comes in, every boat in the harbor rises with it. The old boats that have seen better days are lifted right along with the sleek new ones. Making a manifesting Mount Rushmore allows you to take full advantage of this characteristic.

Making a manifesting Mount Rushmore utilizes the underlying interconnectedness of me, the one consciousness. You have carefully curated four important accomplishments that strongly exemplify your desired state of being. They are interconnected through their representation of your interests, passions, and strengths. Each of the four has the potential to manifest your larger desire, but they do not have to make the lift alone.

The actions, ideas, attitudes, and focus you employ to manifest each of your Mount Rushmore achievements are useful to all four. Your careful selection of form and your best efforts to follow it build your capacity to manifest each of them. And success with any will also continually open you up to investment from people even more qualified to help you grow.

Each of the four ways you have chosen to experience what you desire assists the other. Just as the tide lifts every boat in the harbor, successfully manifesting any one of them makes the other three rise too. Since they all come along for the ride, manifesting one has the effect of manifesting all four.

Making a Manifesting Mount Rushmore Distributes the Responsibilities

Making a manifesting Mount Rushmore separates verbs from nouns in your intentional manifesting. A noun identifies or names a class of people, places, or things, while a verb describes an action, a state, or an occurrence. Nouns speak to who you are, while verbs speak to what you do.

This technique establishes your primary desire as a noun, as something you can <u>be</u>. And it also creates four unique but interrelated verbs which will elicit that noun. For example, wealthy can serve as your state of being, while making lots of money is something you do. You can now give your best efforts to four distinct accomplishments to produce your desired life. None of the four you selected carries the entire weight, though, so you've increased the potential for successfully manifesting your desire by 400 percent.

Manifesting an achievement is, after all, not synonymous with manifesting the state of being usually associated with it. For example, accumulating a million dollars does not guarantee that you'll experience *being* wealthy. Nor does attracting a soulmate assure you of experiencing *being* in love. And having a beach body doesn't guarantee you'll experience *being* fit. There are miserable rich people, lonely married people, and people who remain unsatisfied with their bodies despite having an ideal physique.

To manifest the big stuff, you don't want all the responsibility riding on one accomplishment alone because that's simply not a proven formula for long-term success. There are too many factors out of your control that can limit your ability, for example, to manifest a million dollars. But you're far more likely to manifest "wealth" now that "$1 million" is merely one of four accomplishments you're using to evoke it.

Making a Manifesting Mount Rushmore Lowers the Pressure

It's natural for humans to focus on their weaknesses. When your report card had all As except that one C in algebra, where did you focus your attention? While normal and logical, that approach is actually counterproductive to success. It turns out that focusing on your strengths rather than your weaknesses creates the highest probability of manifesting reality and engaging with it as you desire.

Making a manifesting Mount Rushmore is all about focusing on where your greatest interests and attributes are found. They are each exciting to you. The four accomplishments you select to elicit your desired state of being are things you're passionate about and motivated to cultivate. While your success in each probably won't be a straight-line, upward trajectory, because almost nothing in life is, you won't mind giving your best efforts to accomplish them.

And that makes this technique a pressure-reducer. Making a manifesting Mount Rushmore takes almost all the pressure off of any one of the accomplishments you selected. The more avenues available to manifest your desire, the less weight any of the individual pathways to it must bear. Using this technique puts your eggs in *many* baskets rather than one.

The less burden one individual accomplishment carries to elicit your preferred state of being, the less pressure there is on you and it. You are not beholden to one specific accomplishment to elicit your desired version of reality. You now have four equally important achievements to signify and create the life you desire.

Making a Manifesting Mount Rushmore Mirrors How You Manifest Reality

You and I coordinate the manifestation of your reality—we're of equal importance. Manifesting is a dance between you and me, performed either by default or intentionally each moment you're here. You couldn't manifest your version of reality without me, and your version of reality wouldn't exist without you.

You have the most capable dance partner possible in me, but to intentionally manifest your desired life, you must take the lead. I am, of course, pure possibility. I am the source of all the potential content, all the states of being you desire. You, in turn, get to provide the actions. You get to provide effort; you get to contribute the verbs. Your actions manifest states of being from my infinite possibilities.

You get to pick which state of being is most important to you, and then you get to pick the actions you'll take to evoke it. You get to elicit your noun using verbs, giving your best effort to follow form and manifest it through each of the four accomplishments you selected.

States of being and accomplishments are both critical for manifesting and engaging with more pleasing versions of reality. When trying to manifest their life differently, however, humans often make the mistake of focusing primarily on the verbs. And conversely, sometimes they make the mistake of focusing mainly on nouns at the expense of verbs.

Making a manifesting Mount Rushmore directs you to use nouns and verbs equally. Wealth, love, and health can all be how you exist; they can all be things you experience as who you *are*. This is literal, as in "I am wealth," "I am love," and "I am health," in addition to their use as an adjective, à la "I am wealthy." Using this technique allows my potential to meet your action, which is how the most pleasing parts of your life are always created. Here, you are scripting your actions to match your interests, passions, and strengths. Thus, making a manifesting Mount Rushmore manifests a desired state of being through your concerted efforts.

Technique Eight: Create a Flow State

When to Create a Flow State

Create a flow state when you want to put me, the Quantum Field, on your board of directors. Especially when you want personalized help to actualize very important parts of your life as you truly desire. Use this technique when you want individualized assistance and direction, a personal and unambiguous connection, with me, the one consciousness.

How to Create a Flow State

Hungarian-American psychologist Mihaly Csikszentmihalyi coined the term "flow state." You may have heard it referred to as being in the zone or in the groove. When in a flow state, you literally lose your self in what you're doing. And without your self, we are together again, wholly.

You've probably experienced types of flow states. Holding a newborn child, watching a spectacular sunset, and laughing uproariously are all examples of when a flow state can occur. You lose yourself in the moment, time melts away, and you feel connected and safe. You remember that you are at one with the universe. This technique allows you to create this state intentionally and much more powerfully.

First, select a challenging physical activity. Physical exercise is an easy choice, done in collaboration with your doctor or healthcare provider. Running, brisk walking, yoga, Pilates, biking, stair climbing, lifting weights, hiking, and swimming are good examples. You can also select a non-workout-related physical activity, such as tennis, dancing, pickleball, gardening, basketball, or yard work. Some people even use activities like painting, woodworking, sculpting, drawing, and playing a musical instrument because they involve using your hands. As long as the activity is challenging and requires physical engagement, you can probably use it to create flow states.

Next, learn the best form for performing the physical activity you've selected. The most powerful flow states occur when the challenge level of your activity and your skill level are both high, so it's vital to learn proper form from people performing your physical activity at a high level. Giving your best effort to follow form, over time, builds a high skill level.

Form gives a job to each part of your whole self to fulfill while engaging in this activity. It involves how to engage each muscle and system of your body to perform the activity. Form instructs how to breathe, how to best support your muscles and systems, and even how to think and focus while doing it.

Then, for at least 150 minutes a week, give your best effort to follow form while performing that activity. You do not need to do it perfectly. You simply need to give your best effort to adhere wholly to the form for that activity. Doing your best to follow form instills a skill level, right from the start, capable of creating flow states. With an average of about twenty minutes a day, your skill level will grow over time, and the flow states you create will become more frequent and more powerful.

Here is how you'll know when you're in a flow state:

- You are 100 percent focused in the moment. You are fully present and alive right here, right now.

- You lose your self. You're temporarily untethered from being a distinct time-space event and are connected with me underneath the "water's surface."

- Time disappears. A moment can feel like an hour and an hour can feel like a second.

- Everything makes sense. You spontaneously make deep and rewarding connections.

- The energy connection between thought and action is almost perfect. There is an almost instantaneous flow of communication between the thought and action.

- Giving your best effort to perform the activity as form dictates becomes the reward. The primary value of the activity is found in how present and alive it allows you to be in each moment.

Next, while in a flow state, feel and process whatever feelings you encounter. Don't judge the feelings and don't judge yourself for having them. Simply feel whatever's there and process it physically. As if you're making dough, let the activity knead the feelings out of your muscles as you use them to stay in form.

Then follow painful feelings back to their source by asking yourself, *"What must I believe about myself to feel this way?"* Because painful feelings are shadows cast by incapable beliefs and inadequate ways of engaging with your life, you can follow them back to their source. In this way, painful feelings will lead you to incapable beliefs and inadequate ways of engaging that you can grow into alignment with your desires.

During flow states, you and I will be able to communicate directly about what you've discovered. We can experiment with different perspectives and devise a good engagement plan for this part of your life. I'll help you identify some actions, ideas, attitudes, and focus that can alleviate your pain.

Then, you get to carry all this information back with you from the flow state and follow through on it. It is now an actionable part of your conscious awareness and can inform your decision-making about actions, ideas, attitudes, and focus and your follow-through. You have literally put me on your board of directors, and I'll meet with you as often as you want!

Why Creating a Flow State Helps Your Performance

Creating a flow state is my favorite technique because of how personally it allows us to connect, but that's not the only reason it's such a powerful tool. There are at least four unique ways that a flow state will help your performances. While using this technique won't guarantee your ultimate success, it is the single most effective way to position yourself for the best performances possible.

Creating a flow state:

- Puts you in direct contact with the Quantum Field

- Grows an autotelic focus

- Helps you feel and process feelings

- Presents you with high-quality solutions

Creating a Flow State Puts You in Direct Contact with the Quantum Field

I can't perform your flow-state-inducing activity for you, and I can't give you your best effort to follow form. You get to do those things, and only you can. But I'm always here, always available for personal consultation, whenever you create a flow state. And the direct communication we get to have makes this technique my absolute favorite.

We can correspond personally while you are in a flow state. I'm communicating with you through Greg Kuhn right now, but Greg isn't *required*. You and I are every bit as much of a "we" as Greg and I are, and in a flow state, you and I can share one-on-one. I can be on your board of directors as readily as I am on Greg's.

I appreciate that Greg is committed to helping us connect through his writing and speaking. He is passionate about conveying everything I share with him. Now, with this technique, you can also start your own unique hotline with me. Create flow states for 150 minutes a week and find out for yourself what it's like to have personalized help from me.

When you temporarily take your self offline during a flow state, Energy-You remains because that's the "real" you. In a flow state, we're back together and can communicate instantaneously. And I can even help you manifest and engage with reality even after the flow state is over.

In a flow state, I can give you personal and nonjudgmental feedback about your self, the reality you are manifesting, and your engagement with it. I can help you process your feelings and learn, grow, and change. I can also help you envision and conceptualize new possibilities from what you learn, and I can help you explore new timelines from the perspectives of those new possibilities. And you never have to worry about me having ulterior motives because we are one and the same.

Creating a Flow State Grows an Autotelic Focus

Having an autotelic focus, also called a growth mindset, is incredibly helpful for intentional manifesting. An autotelic focus means you have a powerful desire to learn and know. You're not focused on being perfect; rather, you want to grow. It also means you have a strong commitment to not giving up, even when things get difficult. And finally, an autotelic focus means you have an appropriately modest view of your own importance.

Part of what makes an autotelic focus so valuable is it allows you to enjoy a situation that someone else might hate (like performing a challenging physical activity for 150 minutes a week). That happens best when you're in it for the learning and growth rather than for the outcome. Continuing to give twenty minutes a day of your best effort builds this trait while simultaneously feeding off it.

Focusing on learning and growth tends to lead to success, while pressure to achieve results can stifle it. Fixating on outcomes can add stress to your performances, which dampens creativity and resilience. Keeping yourself attuned to learning and growth, for its own sake, will not guarantee you the exact success you dream of, but it is a potent pathway to it.

An autotelic focus can even help you maintain an appropriate grasp of your importance, which can easily get out of whack and create problems. A direct and immediate connection between us almost always reminds you that you are but one time-space event in the unimaginably vast entirety of the universe. In relation to the rest of material reality, you are less significant than one grain of sand. And at the same time, you are the single most important part of your life because, without you, your reality would not exist.

Creating a Flow State Helps You Feel and Process Feelings

In a flow state, you can exorcize demons such as sadness, guilt, worry, doubt, anger, and regret. Those types of feelings are normal and expected. Such emotions are the shadows of ineffective beliefs, almost all of which you received during childhood, and inadequate engagement, which every human occasionally suffers from. But while feeling them is unavoidable, being tortured by them isn't.

Feelings haunt you when you haven't felt and processed them. When a human tries to stuff, ignore, or pretend they don't have painful feelings, those emotions take residence and remain in their body until they get processed. It's common to worry that feeling your painful feelings will solidify them or make them more real. In actuality, however, it's *not* feeling your feelings that keeps them around.

You become your feelings when you don't feel them and process them. Feeling angry, for example, is ugly enough, but being angry becomes your state of being when you don't process it. That means your anger becomes prompted as much by unprocessed feelings from your past as from what's happening now. You're much more likely to lash out in ways you later regret.

In a flow state, allow yourself to feel any emotion you encounter. Become nonjudgmentally immersed in it. Don't criticize yourself for how you feel. Simply feel and process whatever comes up. Do this so you can follow painful feelings back to their source. Ask yourself, *"What must I believe about myself to feel this way about this part of my life?"*

You have new clarity on your incapable beliefs and new insight into your inadequate engagement. But no matter what, you'll have felt and processed some painful emotions. Painful feelings go away once they're processed, and that's what you want them to do (after you learn from them).

Creating a Flow State Presents You with High-Quality Solutions

I can't tell you what is right for you, but I can definitely point you in the right direction. While you're in a flow state, our communication is almost completely unfiltered. You get accurate, personalized information and help from me. So the solutions to your painful life that emerge are of the highest quality.

For example, let's say that during a flow state, you follow feelings of regret back to a concern that you're an inadequate parent. You can use that information to craft a potential remedy by asking yourself, *"What would allow me to know that I am an adequate parent?"* A good answer would be, *"If my son is honest with me about important things and listens to my advice, that would mean I am an adequate parent."*

Still in your flow state, you can next ask, *"Under what circumstances would my son most likely be honest with me and listen to my advice?"* And your answer might be, *"If I am trustworthy, invested in him, and know what I'm talking about."* Then you could give your best effort to produce those conditions by following through on being as trustworthy, invested, and knowledgeable as you can. While your follow-through would not guarantee the parental adequacy you desire, it is much more likely to do so than knee-jerk responses. That is the type of high-quality solution I can help you find.

The high-quality solutions arising from flow states may not always work exactly as you hope, at least not immediately. But they will reveal other opportunities that were previously hidden. Because flow states are highly likely to identify solutions to incapable beliefs and inadequate engagement, they always further your journey.

You're now well-equipped to engage with your reality with a concentration on learning, growing, and changing. These eight techniques provide an evergreen source of feedback and guidance, enabling you to engage with reality at a high level. At this point, having thoroughly covered intentional manifesting and engagement, I'm going to turn things back over to Greg so he can share how he uses this information.

CHAPTER EIGHT

HOW GREG INTENTIONALLY MANIFESTS AND ENGAGES WITH HIS REALITY

Hello again. Greg here, and I'm back to share how I put everything you've read into use in my life. But first, some quick words about channeling.

I channel information from the Quantum Field during flow states. I create flow states while I run, and this book was channeled that way. But I don't believe I'm necessarily doing anything too unusual because we are all channeling during every moment of our lives.

In each moment, you and I channel the Quantum Field and create our versions of reality. We are literally bringing the Quantum Field to life in each moment. We are serving as conduits for the Field, allowing it to break the surface and become material reality.

What each of us channels, or manifests, is uniquely tailored by our beliefs and our engagement. I can't speak for you, but as a rule, I'm not satisfied with my life being unfulfilling. In meaningful parts of my life, I give my best effort to be fulfilled until that happens.

Because of my commitment to fulfillment, intentional manifesting and engagement is my lifestyle, not something I only do occasionally. I base my life on the blueprint outlined in

Chapters Four, Five, and Six. I do it far from perfectly, but in the most essential parts of my life, I'm always giving my best effort. Because life involves pain, I'm always using those three access points to change my default settings.

The Opportunities Each of Us Have Today

Every day, in each moment, you and I can manifest the wealth, health, love, and anything else we desire. Each opportunity is given to us with no strings attached. It is bestowed upon us simply by opening our eyes and drawing breath. We can take advantage of any or all these opportunities, in each moment of each day, by giving our best effort. And a decision to do that always provides us the best chances of creating and experiencing the outcomes we truly want.

I've learned that the best path to the changes I seek starts with examining how I'm manifesting and engaging with reality. When my life is dissatisfying, which happens often, using a Learn, Grow, Change manifesting focus always leads me to solutions. There are always things I can or need to do to more successfully engage with reality. Sometimes I need to change what I'm doing, and other times I need to give a better effort to what I'm doing. Sometimes I need to put healthier boundaries in place, and other times I need to start better honoring the boundaries already there.

Accepting responsibility for resolving painful versions of reality in this way is not synonymous with accepting blame for them. I know how to blame myself for my pain and beat myself up for it too—and that's something I definitely don't want to get any better at! Instead, it's about accepting responsibility for my fulfillment.

I accept responsibility for fulfillment, prioritizing it over even success or achievement, because manifesting fulfilling versions of reality isn't dependent upon any specific outcomes. Rather, fulfilling versions of reality result from giving my best effort in each moment. So that's always my aim, and it almost always produces the best outcomes anyway.

And to help me do this, I avail myself to the most expert mentorship I can access. I don't rely on someone only because I trust them or because they're familiar to me—they must also know what they're talking about, as demonstrated by verifiable success in their life. And I follow their suggestions.

How I Intentionally Manifested This Book

Now let's connect this handbook directly to my life.

On July 1, 2022, I retired from the Jefferson County, Kentucky, public school system to be a full-time author and speaker. And on August 1, 2022, I officially started writing this book. The book you're now reading shouldered a lot of responsibility—it was a point of entry into my new career.

Well, actually, this book was a point of *reentry*, since I'd been writing and speaking about how to manifest desires since 2012. This book is my eighth, in fact, but my first since 2018. So I was certain of two things on August 1, 2022: I had a lot of new things to say, and I would get them said because I know how to write a book.

To kick-start my second career, I started a podcast called *Manifest the Big Stuff* in January of 2022. On my podcast, I only speak about things I actually do and ideas that really work for me. So once a week, I had been delivering fresh, creative insights about how to manifest your desires and engage successfully with reality.

I'd had a lot of fun reentering the public arena with new content. And in turn, publishing a new podcast episode once a week helped me clarify and update my message. It forced me to learn how to explain my current experiences with manifesting and engaging. My once-a-week publishing schedule created a positive checkmate by requiring me to significantly put myself out there again.

Based on my previous writing experiences and my success with the podcast, I had some reasonable expectations that this book would be easy to write. I knew this book's title, its point of view, the story, and I had an outline. I was excited that a great book was percolating inside me. Past experience informs me that such circumstances can lead to an almost effortless writing experience.

Everything sure appeared to be in place. I envisioned myself, on August 1, starting down a wonderful rabbit hole of writing. I was ready to watch, like a spectator, my pen move across the page as if it had a mind of its own, which had happened many times before.

Let's Get This Party Started!

I began my day, Monday, August 1, around seven a.m. As is my custom, I journaled myself into vibrational alignment with the opportunities I had in each moment to intentionally manifest and engage with my reality that day. I don't try to pump myself up when journaling myself into vibrational alignment, but my inherent excitement for writing this book was evident that morning.

Here's that journal entry:

8/1/22

Getting it done on August 1! Am I ready? I don't know to what extent, but, yes. I am ready to be present in this moment and manifest a version of reality as closely aligned with my desires as I'm capable of seeing and understanding. To start, how about working on Chapter 1 while simultaneously considering it for a podcast episode? Let's see where that takes me! I love being alive! Thank you for this opportunity!

But I didn't write that Monday! Instead, I spent the day doing some yard work that caught my attention when I walked our dogs after breakfast. Working outside was not how I imagined Monday going, but there was no doubt our lawn and foliage benefited from my attention. Since our property looked so much better afterward, I filed Monday under "getting organized before getting productive." I gave myself a mulligan and refocused on getting started the next day.

Tuesday, August 2, also began with me journaling myself into vibrational alignment. Once again, I didn't set out to pump myself up, but excitement and positive expectations were still front and center. Yesterday had obviously been a "get-ready day." Today would see me joyfully roll up my sleeves and get writing!

Here's that journal entry:

8/2/22

Today is downstream, baby! I know what I'm doing—making a podcast and writing a book. And I don't need to swim upstream to do it today. I woke up, I opened my eyes, and the sun was shining. This is officially a day of life. On this planet, here in 3D time-space. How lucky am I? Do I know beyond doubt that I will respond to this day and its opportunities with the precise work ethic I imagine may be required (and am positive is productive)? I don't know. But I do know this: I am taking care with my input today, and I have the opportunity today. Many times throughout. Let's swim downstream!

Not long after writing that, I parked myself in front of my PC to begin writing this book in earnest but felt not one iota of motivation. Undeterred, I switched gears and looked at my next podcast episode, which I'd need to record soon. To my surprise, I had no drive there either; I felt like a flat soda. But rather than berating myself, I got up and started cleaning our house. By the end of the day, I had done no writing, but the house looked great.

Not only had I not begun writing my new book, but my next podcast episode was also a ghost town. That was a bit concerning, considering *Manifest the Big Stuff* had been flowing out of me pretty much effortlessly, once a week, for over six months. I'd had a productive two days, but none of that included new creative content.

On Wednesday, August 3, I reached for my journal before getting out of bed. *Enough playing around,* I thought. Surely, I'd gotten all my organizing and getting ready over with; today would definitely be the day. I was ready to enjoy channeling information from the Quantum Field to create both my new book and my next podcast episode. What I wrote in my alignment journal that morning was short, sweet, and to the point.

Here's that journal entry:

8/3/22

*Let's do it! Let's make something happen! Downstream! Podcast. Book. Let's f***king go!*

To my dismay, though, on Wednesday, I encountered the same doldrums. No excitement, no energy, and no enthusiasm equaled no motivation—I simply didn't want to write. I'd sometimes experienced effortless flow while writing previous books and had reasons to expect the same now. I loved everything about this book and knew it would be a powerful addition to so many readers' libraries. I wanted, and needed, to get it written!

To make matters worse, I was nearing a deadline to create my next episode of *Manifest the Big Stuff*. For the first time in over six months, it was looking like I had nothing to say. After producing a weekly cornucopia of original manifesting content since January, I was experiencing a creative dust bowl.

This was bad!

Self-Doubt Led to a Realization

I spent Wednesday growing increasingly concerned and started doubting the whole plan. Was I just fooling myself? Was I really going to do this? Did I sell my family (and myself) on a pipe dream? After planning for years to transition to a full-time author and speaker, was I fumbling the ball at the goal line?

I'd been doing everything right. I was vibrationally aligning myself each morning. And I was using the eight techniques found in the previous chapter every day to guide my actions, ideas, attitudes, focus, and follow through on those decisions. This book and my next podcast episode should've been a snap for me, so what was wrong?

I went to bed on Wednesday worried, open to answers, and hoping some would arrive soon. And sure enough, the next morning it hit me like a bolt out of the blue! My beliefs were incapable of manifesting a reality supportive of my desires to write this book and become a full-time author and speaker. My feelings of worry and self-doubt were the shadows of incapable beliefs!

The solution was simple because my painful feelings pointed me right toward it: the belief-raising process. The evidence provided by my worry was staring me right in the face and grabbing my attention. My next move was obvious—my painful feelings told me it was time to use the belief-raising process again.

So Thursday morning, August 4, I began using the belief-raising process on my desire to write this book. I followed the instructions exactly as written, as I always do. My initial writing landed me on the emotional perspective of Worry/Nervousness, so that was my starting point.

Even before taking our dogs for a walk, I wrote myself into the next highest emotional perspective on the chart: Frustration/Aggravation. After looking up their definitions, I asked myself, *What must I believe about myself to feel frustrated and aggravated about my desire to manifest this book?*

Frustration/Aggravation made sense to me. Applying those feelings to this situation wasn't a stretch because they fit well. I was easily able to use their definitions to begin feeling annoyed by my inability to achieve my new book. And my irritation was intensified by how important the project was.

After writing about my desire from the perspective of Frustration/Aggravation, I started manifesting this book project from there. I began living my way into that new emotional perspective. And as has always been the case, manifesting from Frustration/Aggravation changed my life in real time. Life did not morph into my ultimate desires for it, but I saw small, immediate improvements in accord with the slightly more empowering emotional perspective.

And although I was feeling frustrated and aggravated about this book, which was far from where I wanted to be, I also felt some authentic excitement for the first time all week. Using the belief-raising process again provided a hint of the success I had been looking for. Although I was still far from the top of the chart, I knew I was applying a powerful solution to my painful life.

The Party Finally Got Started!

If you've never used the belief-raising process, you might say, *"But Greg, frustration and aggravation are hardly improvements at all from where you started. That isn't a positive emotional state, and it's not going to manifest your reality the way you want."* You'd not only be correct, you'd have also highlighted the reason this belief-raising process is so incredibly effective and powerful: it intentionally keeps the improvements minimal.

Sometimes there's hardly a noticeable improvement from one emotional perspective to the next. This allows your subconscious to understand, believe, and embrace the new perspective. Incremental improvements keep you emotionally honest. Because every new perspective is so close to the previous one, your subconscious will allow it to grow your beliefs one small step at a time.

My subconscious has always allowed my beliefs to grow and become aligned with my desires in any area of my life as long as I speak the truth to it emotionally. Even when the next highest emotional perspective is still, technically, a negative one, it will be slightly more aligned than its predecessor. Even when a new perspective doesn't look promising, my writing coaxes out a way to see and understand things that's a bit more empowering.

Frustration/Aggravation is a more forward-looking, self-empowering perspective than Worry/Nervousness. So while my life was still far from what I truly desired, it did improve slightly immediately. My writing revealed, for example, how frustrated I felt about having worked my butt off making a great podcast for almost seven months with seemingly nothing to show for it.

Yes, I feel frustrated, I wrote, *I have good reason to—I've been working like a dog and should have more happening because of it.* While still painful, those authentic feelings were actually a small step in the right direction. They were a minor improvement over my previous worry about being a fraud.

Day by day, I continued writing and working this process. I wrote and lived my way into new emotional perspectives. I slowly but surely moved my way up the Emotional Reference Chart and enjoyed witnessing the form, function, meaning, and value of my life changing in real time. The gradual but noticeable improvements were exciting and motivating.

It was at the emotional perspective of Introspection/Contemplation that things really started taking off for me. I distinctly remember the moment I paused while writing about that perspective and thought, *Holy shit! I'm using the belief-raising process to write a book* (wait for it) *about the belief-raising process! This is all happening exactly as it is supposed to!*

Every bit of it! It blew my mind, quite frankly. Especially considering where I started, it was thrilling to manifest a reality that truly supported my desire to write this book.

In less than 30 days, on August 31, I reached the emotional perspective of Love/Ecstasy. Bear in mind that I was recording episodes a couple weeks in advance, but you can follow my use of the belief-raising process, in real time, on my podcast, *Manifest the Big Stuff*. Start with the episode "It Was Even Better than Originally Desired" and end with "Be Manifested How You Really Want."

By December 1, 2022, I had completed the first draft of everything here except this chapter. It took commitment, effort, and persistence, but I wrote the bulk of this entire book in only three months after using this process to align my beliefs. The editing and polishing process was still ahead, but the belief-raising process made completing the manuscript a downstream operation, which didn't surprise me in the least!

How I Intentionally Manifest and Engage with My Reality

If you don't already know, I'm an avid runner who averages 30–35 miles in a good week. As a Christmas present in 2022, my oldest son, Jordan, gave me a pair of Asics Metaspeed Edges. I usually run in Hoka One One Cliftons, but I was eager to try the Asics because they have carbon fiber plates in their soles.

A carbon fiber plate is a boon to runners because it provides excellent energy absorption *and* energy return. Normally, something can only do one of those things for you. Grass, for example, allows for much better energy absorption than concrete, which is good for your body. On the other hand, concrete gives much better energy return than grass, which helps propel you forward.

I was pumped to try the Asics, so I ran in them the next day. I could definitely tell a difference because I had a deeper reservoir of strength and energy. And afterward, when

I looked at my performance stats, I could also see their impact because I ran farther and faster with less exertion than normal.

At the end of the day, however, running in the Asics was the same as running in my Hokas. The Asics didn't keep me in proper form—I did that. Neither did they give my full effort in each moment—that was also me. I still employed the same movements and breathing and kept the same focus in the moment. Although the Asics gave me some tangible advantages, they did not change the <u>act</u> of running, which is a great metaphor for intentional manifesting and engagement.

Here's what I mean by that.

I Run to Channel from the Quantum Field

The reason I run is to create flow states, during which I channel information directly from the Quantum Field. Running to create flow states is an essential part of how I live my life and an integral part of my writing and speaking. Running is where I "download" a lot of my ideas about intentional manifesting and engagement. Most of what I share with you was originally channeled during flow states.

I do not run to log a certain distance or achieve a specific pace. Nor do I run to shape my body or keep weight off. My runs are not about specific performance objectives at all; rather, they have the simple goal of giving a total effort of mind, body, and spirit in each moment to maintain proper form. Regardless of how far or fast I run, if I give my best effort in each moment to use proper form, it's a successful run.

I've found that giving my best effort to use proper form in each moment of running creates the flow states I seek. Focusing on my performance, however, eventually creates performance anxiety. Ironically, rejecting a performance focus actually elicits far better measurable outcomes anyway. I've achieved the highest levels of distance, pace, health, and physical fitness of my life by focusing solely on my effort.

It doesn't matter if I'm running hills or flat ground, what type of shoes or clothing I wear, whether it's cold or hot outside, or if I have physical pain in my body or not. Such things can definitely affect my performance, but they do not affect my effort unless I allow them to. No circumstance negates my ability to give my best effort in each moment of my run.

Effort really is what it's all about.

You Can't Take the Next Step without Taking This One

It's nearly impossible to manifest better versions of life without first manifesting them as well as you're currently capable. Even when the results are good, without that focus, you'll miss all the feedback. Manifesting your reality as well as you're currently able provides massively helpful information.

The carbon fiber plates provide superior and sustainable energy absorption and return rates, but they don't run *for* me. And neither do the Asics create flow states *for* me. I still get to do all that through my effort. It doesn't matter whether I'm wearing my carbon fiber Asics or my Hokas. Just as it doesn't matter if I'm running up hills, it's cold outside, or my knee is in pain. It's the same process, regardless of my equipment and circumstances.

My beliefs manifest the form, function, meaning, and value of my running reality. They manifest the <u>stage upon which I run</u> and everything associated with it. And, of course, my beliefs are not always aligned with what I want.

I <u>prepare for each run</u> by vibrationally aligning with the opportunities I have in each moment. I do not seek alignment with performance-based outcomes, such as how far and fast to run. And as you might guess, I'm not always naturally excited about the opportunity to run.

Being fully present and alive in each moment and giving my best effort to follow form is <u>how I run</u>—not by achieving or maintaining a certain pace nor by running a certain distance. And as we all know, my best effort will look different from day to day.

I Get To Intentionally Manifest My Desires

Growing my reality in any other part of my life works the same way. In every area, each moment provides me the opportunity to intentionally manifest and engage with my reality. And by focusing on my effort rather than the results, I create the best outcomes possible for me at that time.

We see this play out often. Having lots of money doesn't, in and of itself, *make* someone experience being wealthy. Nor does having a soulmate *give* you the experience of love with absolute certainty. And being illness-free alone doesn't *make* anyone experience being healthy either. Yes, it's easier to manifest wealth with lots of money, love with a soulmate, and health with no illness, but those things, by themselves, are not guarantees.

As with my Asics, I'll take advantage of and even intentionally create any help I can get. Carbon fiber plates, lots of money, a soulmate, and no illnesses are not only incredibly helpful tools, but they're also pleasing in and of themselves. They are all measurable outcomes that can readily be demonstrated and identified, which makes them important signifiers. And creating important signifiers is valuable for public-facing performance artists like us.

Being fit, being wealthy, being in love, and being healthy, on the other hand, are things I *am*, things I can experience *being*. They are all states of being, none of them limited to or dependent on one defining characteristic. States of being are aiming points—they are among the primary reasons to cultivate important signifiers.

Desired states of being can be difficult to manifest without some of their important signifiers, which is why we want them so badly. And yet, desired states of being are not dependent upon any one signifier or achievement. In fact, my states of being are often just as responsible for the presence of important signifiers in my life as the signifiers are for my states of being.

I Am Currently Manifesting All My Desires

Yes, you read that correctly. I am currently manifesting *all* my desires—to the extent possible for me right now. How do I know that for certain? Because in every area of my life, I am giving my best effort:

- To grow my incapable inherited beliefs into alignment with my desires

- To align myself vibrationally each morning with the opportunities I'm provided in every moment to intentionally manifest and engage with my reality

- And to let my engagement with reality be guided by a commitment to learn, grow, and change

Staking the claim that I manifest my desires right from the start is valuable for three important reasons. First, it's affirming and feels good. I'm not trying to fool myself into thinking my life is already where I want it to be. I'm simply recognizing my efforts to intentionally manifest it. I'm authentically acknowledging that I'm manifesting the best versions of my life currently possible.

Second, it keeps the focus squarely on giving my best effort, where it needs to be, rather than the outcomes. I'm being factual when recognizing that all I'll ever be able to do is give my best effort. Even when I eventually manifest this part of my life as I really want, I'll be doing it the same way—by giving my best effort. Giving my best effort is, in fact, the act of manifesting my reality intentionally.

Third, and perhaps most importantly, staking this claim helps me learn, grow, and change. Giving my best effort to intentionally manifest my desire teaches me almost everything I need to know to take the next step. My reality always provides precise, essential feedback about the adequacy of my efforts and where I'm directing them. But I can't access those lessons without being completely invested in giving my best effort.

You Manifest Your Desire the Moment You Start Doing So Intentionally

Here's an example of what I'm talking about straight from my hometown of Louisville, KY. Let's say my desire is to ride a horse in a race at Churchill Downs, and my starting point is that I've never even ridden a horse—I'm starting from scratch. That's not an impossible thing to manifest, assuming I have access to a racehorse that I'd be allowed to ride.

Since I'm starting at square one, the first thing I need to learn is how to mount a horse and sit in the saddle. That's a baby step, right? But once I do it, I am manifesting my desire. Not at the level I ultimately aspire to, of course, but as well as I'm currently able.

As soon as I've mastered mounting and sitting, I'll be on to step two: learning how to control a horse and ride it. But I can't learn step two without first mastering step one. This means step one, learning to mount and sit, is the single most important part of manifesting my desire to ride in a race.

If I tried jumping straight to step two without first learning to mount and sit on a horse, I wouldn't have the proper foundation. I would have missed out on learning things essential for controlling and riding a horse, so success with step two would be less likely. And don't even think about jumping right to the final step, riding a horse in a race, without having mastered step one. What a disaster that would be!

Thus, for all intents and purposes, mastering step one manifests my desire because step one <u>is</u> the most important step. When I'm on step one, that's the best version of my desire I'm currently capable of manifesting. And all that will be true about every step when I'm on it.

You've Always Manifested and Engaged. Now You're Doing It Intentionally

Judging your success based on the results at each step isn't helpful anyway and can actually be counterproductive. Keeping an autotelic focus, a growth mindset, requires you to treat every outcome as a formative assessment. Don't ever "call it," because it's never the <u>final</u> result. We are always a work in progress, and so is our life.

Keeping my results of every step in perspective helps prevent them from wielding too much authority. Why would I assign so much importance to any outcome when there are always people out there exceeding what I've done? Even when I nail it, there are people so successful they'd gasp and ask, *"What the hell went wrong?"* if they got my results.

For example, while I'm raising the roof about <u>riding</u> a horse in a race at Churchill Downs, there will be jockeys who are only satisfied with <u>winning</u> that race. But I'm not doing anything wrong by "only" trying to manifest riding a horse in a race rather than trying to win. This is my life, and I'm manifesting my personal desires, not anyone else's, and my personal desires are the grandest ones I currently dare to dream.

After riding a horse in a race, however, it wouldn't take long before I would want to be among the top three finishers in one. Then, after I manifested that, I'd start wanting to win one. Your capacity grows based on what you learn. As your capacity increases, so do the versions of reality you're able to manifest. And as the reality you manifest becomes more aligned with your true desires, those desires will grow once again.

At the end of the day, when your life is finally aligned with your true desires for it, you'll still be saying the same things about it as when you began:

"I am giving my best effort to manifest and engage with reality in this part of my life. I am manifesting the best version of reality possible for me right now and engaging with it as successfully as I can. And thus, I am intentionally manifesting and engaging with my reality right now."

Don't wait until you reach your ultimate manifesting goals before recognizing what you're doing. Give yourself credit, right from the start, for giving your best effort. Staking that claim will help you master the step you're on, take the next one, and, eventually, reach your objectives.

What Drives Me to Intentionally Manifest and Engage with My Reality?

I am interested in growing my beliefs, aligning myself with my opportunities, and delivering the best performances I'm capable of so that I can create versions of reality more aligned with my desires. And my desires are not really so fantastic. In fact, I'm not trying to be cheeky when I say:

- I don't want to walk on water, unless there's ice on a pond.

- I don't want to fly, unless I'm in an airplane.

- I don't want to turn things into gold, unless I'm selling books.

In theory and practice though, fantastic manifestations are possible. Thank goodness, because I've needed reality-defying manifestations before. For example, I was once six months away from bankruptcy, foreclosures, and lifelong debt, but I manifested my way out of all of it. I've written and talked a lot about that part of my life because it gave birth to what I do now.

Today however, I'm grateful for my more down-to-earth desires to manifest intimacy with my spouse, connection with my sons, wealth from my work, cooperation with my neighbors, professional opportunities, collaboration with partners, peace of mind, satisfaction, success, and, most of all, fulfillment. My opportunities to intentionally create and engage with reality that way get me out of bed each day.

What drives me to make a lifestyle out of intentionally manifesting and engaging with my reality? It comes down to three simple things.

First, since I'm going to perform on a stage set by my beliefs in each moment anyway, I might as well give my best effort to align my beliefs with my desires. Why wouldn't I? I'm going to be performing on the stage they set either way.

Second, since I'm going to be present in each moment, I may as well prepare myself to take advantage of the opportunities each offers me to intentionally manifest and engage with reality. Why wouldn't I align myself vibrationally with those opportunities? They're coming my way in each moment, whether I'm prepared for them or not.

And third, since I'm going to be performing publicly in each moment today, I might as well choose actions, ideas, attitudes, and focus that are likely to help me succeed and then follow through on them. Why wouldn't I do that? There is no way to hide from the results of my engagement with reality, after all.

We're Going to Be Here Anyway, Right?

Since, fair or not, people will evaluate me based on my public-facing performances, I may as well intentionally manifest and engage with my entire life. Truth is, sometimes it's hard not to judge *myself* on my results. There really is no way to escape it, so I might as well embrace it and turn it into motivation.

Since each moment gives me the opportunity to give my best effort, each moment is my stage. I can't opt out of these oncoming opportunities, so I may as well be vibrationally aligned with them. And since I'm going to perform publicly in each moment (since even choosing to hide is a type of performance), I might as well give my best effort.

Please Help Me Be of Value to You

Another thing that drives me to keep intentionally manifesting is connections with other intentional manifesters like you. Helping you become the architect of your life, as you've always known is possible, is incredibly motivating for me. I always write and speak with you in mind, and my intent is always to provide you with actionable solutions to life's challenges.

To that end, please join my free manifesting group on Facebook called "Manifest the Big Stuff, with Greg Kuhn: Creating Our Realities Together" Each month, you get exclusive content only available for members of my FB group.

Each month, I share thoughts, ideas, or lessons I've channeled from the Quantum Field during my time spent in flow states, an entry from my morning alignment journal, some highlights from how I'm engaging with my reality, and entries from my belief-raising journal. You can count on fun, educational, and personal messages, plus you get to interact with a like-minded community of fellow intentional manifesters, all interested in becoming more intentional architects of our life.

Please sign up today and become a part of this amazing manifesting community!

Acknowledgments

This book wouldn't have been possible without the encouragement and feedback of my wife, Shawn Marshall. I am constantly motivated by her work ethic, confidence, and fortitude as a successful visual artist and teacher. When Shawn speaks, I listen.

My youngest son, Logan Kuhn, also played a valuable role in this book's creation as he has helped me with my podcast, *Manifest the Big Stuff*, advised me on social media and talked through many of my ideas with me. And I continue to be inspired by my other three sons, Jordan Kuhn, Will Kuhn, and Garrett Barry, whose input informs my spiritual and personal growth.

Thank you, as well, to Jeannette Maw, Tracey Curran, and Lynn Nice for their feedback, encouragement, and nudges while I wrote this book.

ABOUT THE AUTHOR

Greg Kuhn is a Manifesting Coach, specializing in manifesting the big stuff! Successful health, fitness, wealth, family, marriage, career, and relationships are all examples of what Greg focuses on - your most important desires. To contact Greg, visit his website: www .ManifesttheBigStuff.com

A professional educator, coach, writer, speaker, and podcaster, Greg has been teaching people how to change their beliefs and manifest the reality they truly desire since 2013. Using a method forged in the fires of personal and professional disaster, Greg teaches you how to lead your subconscious (by speaking its native tongue) to change the reality you manifest. And he shows you how to sit in the captain's chair, assuming your role as the CEO of your life. Which all results in truly aligning your beliefs, engaging more successfully with reality, and finally manifesting your most important desires.

Watch Greg's podcast, Manifest the Big Stuff, along with other life-changing content, on his YouTube Channel: https://www.youtube.com/@manifestthebigstuff

And listen to Manifest the Big Stuff on Apple Podcasts, Spotify, Google Podcasts, Stitcher, and almost anywhere else you can listen to podcasts.

Engage with Greg via the links below:

Greg's Free Facebook Manifesting Group: https://www.facebook.com/groups/manifes tthebigstuff

Greg's Free Quantum Thoughts Newsletter: https://manifestthebigstuff.com/newslett
er/

Book Greg to Speak at Your Event: https://manifestthebigstuff.com/speaking/

Greg's LinkedIn: https://www.linkedin.com/in/greg-kuhn-a058913a/

Greg's Twitter: @KuhnGregory

Greg's Instagram: @gregoryskuhn1967

ALSO BY GREG KUHN

All of Greg's books are available on Amazon and/or Audible

<u>Why Quantum Physicists Don't Get Fat</u>

Learn how to see yourself, your body, and your reality in new ways that help you gain the body you desire! Available in paperback and Kindle from Amazon and as an audiobook from Audible.

<u>Why Quantum Physicists Do Not Fail</u>

Using everyday language and "street-level" instructions, this book will have you back on track in no time! Available in paperback and Kindle from Amazon and as an audiobook from Audible.

<u>Why Quantum Physicists Do Not Suffer</u>

Learn a great secret you can start using right now to minimize, or even end, your suffering! Available in Kindle from Amazon.

Why Quantum Physicists Create More Abundance

What does science say about the law of attraction? Is it real? Can it be explained or verified? Yes! Available in Kindle from Amazon.

How Quantum Physicists Build New Beliefs

By learning to speak your subconscious' native tongue, you will truly grow your beliefs into alignment with your desires! Available in paperback and Kindle from Amazon and as an audiobook from Audible.

Why Quantum Physicists Play "Grow a Greater You"

By turning to new paradigms from Quantum Physics, Greg has forged a simple, but powerful, roadmap to manifest reality as you truly desire! Available in paperback and Kindle from Amazon and as an audiobook from Audible.

The 30-Minute Soulmate

Whether you're in a relationship now or not, you will find solutions as you learn to manifest, and be, a soulmate! Available in paperback and Kindle from Amazon.